COACHING
WISDOM

Dedication

To Megan and Grace, always.

*To all the teachers, coaches, and mentors who invest their time
and care deeply about helping others become their best.*

Published by Sellers Publishing, Inc.

Copyright © 2012 Michael Harrity
All rights reserved.

Sellers Publishing, Inc.
161 John Roberts Road, South Portland, Maine 04106
Visit our Web site: www.sellerspublishing.com • E-mail: rsp@rsvp.com

ISBN 13: 978-1-4162-0655-2
e-ISBN: 978-1-4162-0734-4
Library of Congress Control Number: 2011935644

10 9 8 7 6 5 4 3 2 1

Printed and bound in United States of America.

Photo credits: Scotty Bowman: Detroit Red Wings archives; Anson Dorrance: UNC Athletic
Communications; Tony Dungy: Indianapolis Colts; Sue Enquist: UCLA Athletics; Dan Gable:
University of Iowa; Dick Gould: Stanford University Department of Athletics; Lou Holtz: Mike
Bennett, Lighthouse Imaging; Andrea Hudy: Kansas Athletics, Inc.; Tom Osborne: NU Media
Relations; Don Shula: Miami Dolphins; George Stanich: UCLA Athletics; Brad Stevens: John
Fetcho; Frosty Westering: Frosty Westering; John Wooden: UCLA Athletics

COACHING WISDOM

CHAMPION COACHES AND THEIR PLAYERS SHARE SUCCESSFUL LEADERSHIP PRINCIPLES

How *TONY DUNGY, LOU HOLTZ, ANDREA HUDY, DON SHULA, JOHN WOODEN,* and Other Top Coaches Inspired Their Teams to Greatness

Mike Harrity

FOREWORD BY *BRAD STEVENS*   PREFACE BY *LOU HOLTZ*

SELLERS
PUBLISHING

CONTENTS

ACKNOWLEDGMENTS

Without the care, love, and generosity of so many people who took the time to help me with no thought of anything in return, this project would not have been possible. To all of you, I give my most sincere and heartfelt appreciation.

So many contributed to my dream of telling the stories in this book — too many to name, but you know who you are. There are some I feel compelled to single out.

First and foremost, I give my deepest gratitude to the late Coach John Wooden, the first person who believed in my project and gave of his time to help me.

To the coaches, Scotty Bowman, Anson Dorrance, Tony Dungy, Sue Enquist, Dan Gable, Dick Gould, Lou Holtz, Andrea Hudy, Tom Osborne, Don Shula, Brad Stevens, Frosty Westering, John Wooden, and the men and women who played on their teams, thank you for sharing your time and wisdom. I am inspired by your trust and generosity.

My wife, Megan, and daughter, Grace, sacrificed so much time with their husband and daddy in support of my research and writing. Also, Megan, your expertise helped shape our book. While the cover states that I'm the author, this book was truly a Team Harrity effort.

To my trusted advisers and dear friends, Lake Dawson, Tom Thomas, Danny Manning, Justin Bauman, Ted Leland, and Leah and Bob Hemenway, thank you for your wisdom, loyalty, and support.

Marilyn Allen, so much more than my agent, believed in me from the first time we spoke. Your enthusiasm helped fuel me throughout the process — thank you.

My deep appreciation to Ronnie Sellers, founder and president of Sellers Publishing, whose vision led to our book on coaching wisdom.

To Mark Chimsky, who guided me through the editing process with a firm and caring hand, helping me find "my voice" as he pushed me to make our content the strongest it could be. I am honored to have worked with you.

To Renee Cooley, the best proofreader in the business.

To George Corsillo, for doing such a great design for this book.

To Charlotte Cromwell for her production expertise. And to the entire team at Sellers Publishing. Ronnie, you have a great staff. I hope you are happy with the finished product that is *Coaching Wisdom*.

To all those who supported the project in a variety of vital ways: Jerry I. Porras, John C. Maxwell, Jeff Chadiha, Sam Farmer, my father-in-law Dan Brent, Gale and Ardie Sayers, Bernie Kish, Bob LaMonte, Mike Rivera, Brad Thorson, Darrell Stuckey, Brandon Martin, Mike Gavin, Anne Hackbart, Jack Krasula, Donna McCleerey, Jan Partain, Larry Baden, Malcolm Gibson, Patti Phillips, Curtis Hollomon, Brett and Brian Haskell, Amanda Higley, Weston Pletcher and Kyle West.

Thank you to all of the media relations professionals who helped me set up interviews and provided photos.

Thank you to my mom, Oknan, for spending time with Grace on many weekends so I could focus on writing, and dad, John, for offering the eagle eye that only the most well-read person I know could offer.

To the student-athlete development team at The University of Kansas, I wish you continued excellence in your work supporting and empowering Jayhawks.

And finally, to my new team and the student-athletes at the University of Notre Dame, thank you for believing in me. I am blessed with the opportunity to join you and I'm committed to bringing my best to you every day.

FOREWORD

First and foremost, I have no business being mentioned in this book. However, I am honored to have been included amongst the terrific coaches in *Coaching Wisdom*. I have a great deal of admiration for leaders in any industry who continually strive to improve themselves, through both up and down times. Early in my career as an assistant coach, I learned that the best never rest — and they are always trying to stay ahead with regard to thinking, learning, and growing. With *Coaching Wisdom*, I'm excited that more people will learn about the methods of coaches like John Wooden, Tom Osborne, and Tony Dungy — all of whom got the most out of their teams, and were meticulous in their preparation and unwavering commitment. If you want to know how these coaches got the best from their personnel and teams, you'll find out here. I feel humbled and honored to be included. They have inspired me — and I think they'll do the same for you.

— Brad Stevens, *head coach, men's basketball at Butler University*

PREFACE

A good coach can bring out qualities in players that they might not even know they have. Each coach has his or her own style. I always paid attention to how other coaches treated their players — what they did to get good results and what they did that produced the opposite effect. I believe that process had a lot of influence on my own coaching skills and it taught me how to help my players get better every day. For example, one of the things I learned and that I tell other coaches is, "You want to get a winning effort from an individual? Criticize the performance, never the performer."

When Mike Harrity asked if he could interview me for this book and told me what *Coaching Wisdom* was about, I said *yes* right away. I was happy to contribute some of my own experiences and to know that other coaches would be sharing what they did to make their teams champions — not just on the court or on the field — but in life, because that's where it really counts most of all.

I think Mike's book will help readers learn about what goes on before and after the team is actually playing — the effort that goes into building confidence and setting standards and expectations. Coaches will learn a lot from this book, and so will athletes. In fact, I think there are lessons here that everybody can use. I hope you enjoy *Coaching Wisdom* and I hope you'll do what you can — whether as a coach or a spectator — to support your local college teams.

— Lou Holtz, *national championship-winning football coach*

Chapter 1

CREATING A CARING ENVIRONMENT

"PEOPLE DON'T CARE HOW MUCH YOU KNOW,
UNTIL THEY KNOW HOW MUCH YOU CARE."
— PRESIDENT THEODORE ROOSEVELT

What sets championship-level coaches apart? What do athletes remember about their coaches? In nearly every interview I conducted with top coaches, many of whom had earned numerous championships at the highest level, it was apparent that they care deeply about their athletes and find many ways to communicate this. Former Nebraska Cornhusker strong safety Jim Pillen is still amazed today when he remembers how Coach Tom Osborne called him by name on the third day of freshman practice in 1974, despite having a roster of 235 men. Coach Anson Dorrance, the chieftain of the University of North Carolina women's soccer dynasty, takes the time to write each of his seniors a heartfelt letter as they head into their championship game. By asking questions on the sideline about life outside of sports, Coach Tony Dungy made an intentional effort to forge personal connections with his Indianapolis Colts players.

The leadership principles and guidance in this book apply not only to the world of sports, but to business and daily life. Each strategy that gives you a competitive edge in the sports arena will also help you become better business leaders and human beings. We start with the art of creating a caring environment, because it is the foundational building block of all other principles for success to come.

As a coach, you are expected to know your sport. You are expected to develop practice strategies, provide instruction on technique, analyze the competition, and give motivational speeches. Caring about your athletes is probably not outlined explicitly in your job description. Yet caring about your athletes is arguably the most important thing you can do as a coach. When you are coaching, you have the unique opportunity to positively impact the hearts, minds, and performances of your athletes by reminding them that they have value. Show them that you think they are important. Demonstrate consistently that you care. And it may just win you a championship.

> ## "REMEMBER THAT A PERSON'S NAME IS TO THAT PERSON THE SWEETEST AND MOST IMPORTANT SOUND IN ANY LANGUAGE."
> ### — DALE CARNEGIE

Make an effort to learn and remember a person's name. If you are someone who has trouble with this, you are not alone. Keeping names straight might be particularly challenging if you have high turnover among athletes or carry a big roster. But don't use "I'm not good with names" as an excuse. Recognize the importance of knowing the names of all the people you're leading. Commit them to memory. Develop strategies to pair names and faces with unique facts about each individual. Use photo rosters or flash cards. Quiz yourself. Your efforts will pay off when you can address each and every person on your team by name with confidence. The message that you care about them will come through loud and clear. And when they know you care, they will work that much harder for you.

For Tom Osborne, coach of three national championship–winning football teams at the University of Nebraska, and now the Athletics Director there, the effort to care was always intentional. "I think that it does make a point that we tried to make sure all of our players understood that there was no particular pecking order in our concern for them. We tried to make sure that they understood that each player was as important as the other. Now, some were more important to us winning a game on a Saturday afternoon, but in terms of their academics, their family, their overall well-being, we wanted to make sure that they felt valued and understood that we cared about them."

How often are you truly in the moment when you are having a casual conversation with one of your athletes? These days, the distractions and interruptions of technology can make it extra challenging to focus on someone standing right in front of us. We can become so caught up in what happened earlier or what's about to happen that we miss what's going on in the immediate here and now. When you are talking with your team members, stay present. This sounds simple. It isn't. Try to remember the last time you drove your car or ate a meal without multitasking. If it was this week, well done. If you can't think that far back, you're not alone. Practice having mindful conversations. When you ask a member of your team a question, pause and genuinely listen for the answer. An effective open-ended question for learning more about people is, "What's new?" This allows them to share whatever is of most interest to them at that particular moment. Another way to do this is to ask each athlete to complete a survey that includes questions about his or her interests. If you do this, be sure to actually read the answers. But pay close attention now — your job isn't over once you've listened. The next part is just as important. You need to remember what was said and follow up about it at a later time. You might be amazed at how much this will mean to people. If you have any doubts, think about a time recently when someone asked you a question about

COACHING WISDOM

"Coach Osborne showed me that he cared about me and valued me. After that day, I'd run through a brick wall for him."
— Jim Pillen

something personal to you, beyond just, "How's it going?" Consider how that felt. When you take the time to ask, listen, and follow up, your team members will feel important, and they will know you care.

Coaches who genuinely care share something else in common: they have a sincere interest in seeing their athletes succeed in life, a concern that goes way beyond athletic performance. Take Brad Stevens, for example. He has achieved at the highest level of college basketball. As the head coach of the Butler basketball team, he won more games in his first three seasons than anyone in NCAA Division I history, going 89–15. His Bulldogs also made back-to-back Final Fours, finishing as the national runner-up in 2010 and 2011. But that's not what matters most to Stevens. He says, "If we're not focused on these guys 40 years from now, [if] we're just focused on what they can do on the court, then it's not going to be as fulfilling, it's not going to be as meaningful. To be quite honest, the games don't matter if you turn them on five years from now, rewatch how you got to the Final Four, and four of [your players] haven't graduated or are out of work. We want these guys to find great success after this [so they'll have] a greater sense of pride down the road. My wife's mom died of cancer at 54, and the priest said, 'Life is not measured in terms of years, but in terms of meaningfulness.' You keep that in mind whenever you're doing anything with your guys. How meaningful is it if you don't have those relationships when they leave? You can win all you want, but it just doesn't matter if you don't have that."

Build relationships with your athletes. Care about each one of them regardless of his or her athletic performance or winning potential. Take the time to learn about their interests outside of sports. Winning the Super Bowl isn't what made Tony Dungy the best coach that punter Hunter Smith ever had. It was the genuine connection his coach initiated — a responsibility Dungy takes very seriously. "You may not touch everybody individually, every day," says Dungy, "but I always made the effort to take a sincere interest in every guy on our team, to find out what's important to them, how they're doing, ask about their families. I really enjoy that."

"THEY MAY FORGET WHAT YOU SAID, BUT THEY WILL NEVER FORGET HOW YOU MADE THEM FEEL."
— CARL W. BUECHNER

Did you keep in touch with any of your favorite coaches or teachers? How many of your former players have stayed in contact with you? If winning is all that matters to you as a coach, you may be guilty of treating your athletes like interchangeable parts. This might win you a championship or two, but it is not necessarily the road to a long, successful coaching career. Coaches who form long-lasting relationships with their athletes are priming themselves and their teams for sustainable success by setting a caring tone. And when coaches care, teammates tend to care about each other, too. This is true in business and life, as well as sports. Have you considered the impact generated by creating a caring environment on your team? Here are a few highlights: When the competition is on the line, not only are your athletes fighting to win for themselves, they are fighting that much harder to win for their coach and their teammates. When you ask them to run sprints at 6:00 a.m., they work hard with minimal complaints because they trust your training regimen. If you ask them to take on a lesser or different role, they accept change more readily because they believe you have the team's best interest at heart. Caring comes naturally for many people who seek careers in coaching, yet often coaches worry that they will enable their athletes to become "soft" through too much caring. Don't mistake caring for coddling. They are two very different approaches. One of the greatest coaches of all time was a master at caring for his athletes while providing tough discipline.

Legendary coach John Wooden relished the strong relationships formed with his players during his 51 years as a head coach leading young men on high school and college basketball teams. Wooden's coaching stretch at UCLA from 1948–75 gained him the most acclaim during his career. His teams won a still unmatched 10 national championships, including seven consecutively from 1966–73. In 2009,

Sporting News Magazine asked 118 Hall of Famers, championship coaches, and other experts to help determine the top 50 coaches of all time, across all sports. Wooden topped the list. But the wins and championships weren't what Wooden thought about most during the decades after he retired. During a visit I made to his home nearly 30 years after he coached his last game (a national championship win against Louisville in 1975), Wooden didn't hesitate to answer my question, "As a coach, what are you most proud of?" "People may have a hard time believing it, but I believe it now and I remember thinking it when I retired — that I'm more proud of [the fact] that my players go ahead and graduate and have led successful lives, practically all of them, than I am that they won several championships," Wooden said, a smile creasing his face as he looked over at a stack of file folders filled with letters and cards from former players. "As time goes by, it pleases me that I get a lot of letters and phone calls and poems from them."

In fact, while I sat with Wooden in his den, former UCLA All-American and NBA Hall of Famer Bill Walton called to sing his coach a song, a frequent routine according to Wooden. Walton is perhaps the best example of a team member on the receiving end of Wooden's loving yet strict discipline. Wooden enjoyed recounting an interaction involving Walton, a sometimes stubborn college

COACHING WISDOM

"People ask me, 'What was so great about John Wooden?' And as I look back, yes, he was a great coach. He gave great pep talks and great practices. But that's not what I remember. What I remember is him as a person. He was so much more than a coach. Coach Wooden was such an example of sincerity and honesty that I wanted to be like him. We weren't just players to him. We were people he cared about. He got within you. And you believed in him." — Ed Ehlers student-athlete with strong convictions, and his decision to grow a beard. A beard or long hair wouldn't fly on a team coached by Wooden, and Walton knew that. He showed up to practice and told Wooden it was his right to have a beard. Wooden remembered his response. "I asked Bill if he strongly believed that," Wooden said. "He did. I told him, 'I respect you for having strong beliefs and sticking by them, I really do. We're going to miss you, Bill.'" Wooden grinned. "He shaved it off that day."

Forming lifelong relationships is not an easy task. You cannot take a checklist approach to this. What you can do, however, is consistently be accessible to your team members. After all, think about what makes a good parent: he or she probably won't have all the right answers or always do the right thing at the right time, but the key to creating a loving, nurturing environment is often just being present. The same is true with being a good coach. Make yourself available to your team members. Don't simply be around when you have to be around — go above and beyond. Without a doubt, it will be noticed and appreciated. During my interviews with coaches, this was a consistent theme.

Matt Howard believes that a big key to the Butler men's basketball program's success is the fact that Brad Stevens considers them family. When a player phones on a weekend, and Stevens, who is with his wife, Tracy, son, Brady (5 years old during the 2011 Final Four run) and daughter, Kinsey (2 years old during the 2011 Final Four run), takes the call, he is simply stepping away from one family member to be of help to another.

"The door is always open, and when you have somebody who cares about you, who wants to learn what makes you go, what makes you tick, it helps us want to buy into what he's saying, it makes us want to work for him," says Howard, the mop-haired All-Conference power forward and three-time Academic All-American who Stevens said perfectly embodies the principles and values of the Butler program. "It wasn't fake interest; you could tell that he actually cared about you and wanted you to do well. He emphasizes academics and wants to make sure we're a complete person, not just a basketball player. At the same time, it benefits [Stevens] knowing how to talk to us, how to motivate us, how to push us to our maximum."

Forming lasting bonds is easier when your athletes know you are accessible. University of Kansas head strength and conditioning coach Andrea Hudy (pronounced HOO-dee) has nine national championship rings. She is a maverick in her field, a female blazing a trail in a male-dominated profession. And she quickly earns the respect of the athletes who work with her. What's her secret? She is at the top of her field when it comes to knowledge, of course, but more than that, she is accessible beyond what the job requires.

As I sat in her office one morning, Cole Aldrich arrived dressed and ready for a workout. Aldrich, the 2010 first-round pick of the NBA's Oklahoma City Thunder, had just finished his rookie season a few weeks before. He could have been anywhere in the world, and he came back to see his old college strength coach. Why here? Why Hudy?

"When I came [to KU as a freshman], I was baby fat and all that, but she helped me slim down and get stronger," Aldrich says. "But more than that, ever since I got here, we've played around and gave each other heck, whether it was in the weight room or just stopping by. To have somebody in the program like that is huge. Some of the guys look up to her like a second mom."

COACHING WISDOM

"With Andrea Hudy, the trust is there. From day one, she just has a way about her. You are having fun, joking around in a good way [and] getting challenged. Most athletes in college are super competitive people. It makes you focus on what you are doing; all the while you are getting your butt kicked, you don't really mind because you are getting better in the end. That's really how it goes with Hudy."   — Sue Bird,
Two-time National Champion at UConn, two-time
WNBA Champion, two-time Olympic Gold Medalist

While Hudy has a strong ability to strike the balance between fun and work with her athletes, what sets her apart is her consistent and care-filled effort to make time for them, even after their collegiate careers are over. She takes her role as a coach very seriously.

"My parents were both teachers and coaches, so I grew up sitting at the table listening to my mom and dad talk about their students, what worked to reach a kid, what didn't," says Hudy, whose four siblings are all teachers and coaches at either the junior high or high school level. "I think of my family every day and what they've taught me about being an educator. Can I teach somebody something that will last a lifetime? A big part of that is simply being available and letting them know that they can ask questions and you're there to help them get better. They could be the worst athlete in the world, and I care if they get better. They could be the best athlete in the world, and I care that they get better."

"THERE ARE TWO WAYS OF SPREADING LIGHT: TO BE THE CANDLE OR THE MIRROR THAT REFLECTS IT."
— EDITH WHARTON

Are you willing to step out of the spotlight so that those you lead can shine? In competitive arenas, it can be difficult to extract one's own ego from the process of helping others develop their talents and skills. Truly great coaches are not afraid to guide and encourage others to achieve success that may even surpass their own accomplishments. One of the biggest truths in leadership is this: helping others shine takes nothing away from you. In fact, when your team members perform at high levels, it only serves to make you look good. And as a coach, you have all kinds of opportunities to allow your team members to shine. Look for those moments when you can provide encouragement, or "put-ups," as Hall of Fame college football coach Frosty Westering calls verbal affirmations that lift others up.

A common assumption is that most athletes are already extraordinarily confident and don't need or deserve put-ups. We shouldn't stroke their egos, right? Wrong! This is a false assumption. Take a minute to think about the critiques you hand out on a regular basis as a coach. That's your job. And if you're doing your job well, your team members hear a lot of feedback, most of it corrective. Many athletes are starving for affirmation. And a little affirmation can go such a long way. It comes back to creating a caring culture. When your team members feel valued and know exactly what qualities, skills, talents, and behaviors you value in them, they are buoyed by that and will be more apt to perform their best.

In the North Carolina women's soccer program, every young woman who has played for Head Coach Anson Dorrance during the past 32 years has sought the ultimate put-up — the senior letter.

Dorrance's program has won 21 national championships in his 33 years as head coach. His career record is 728 wins, 44 losses, and 26 ties. His program has been so dominant, in fact, that when asked in 1997 by a *Football News Magazine* writer what it was like for North Carolina to have a team other than men's basketball being the preseason number-one ranked team in the country, North Carolina's Hall of Fame men's basketball coach Dean Smith answered, "This is a women's soccer school, we're just trying to keep up with them."

Even with all those wins, most former players will tell you that their senior letter from Dorrance is what means the most to them. Cat Reddick Whitehill is one of the most accomplished players to ever put on the Tar Heel soccer jersey, having been a part of two national championships and winning the Hermann Trophy as the top college player in the country during her senior year. Her favorite memory from her time at Carolina is the senior letter. She says, "I keep it in a special book that has all the poems my dad has written to me every Valentine's Day through the years."

Dorrance came up with the idea for the senior letter when he read about a one-time football coach at the University of Chicago during their heyday. A reporter asked the coach after he had won the national championship, "What do you think of your team?"

"His answer was wonderfully profound," Dorrance says. "He said, 'I'll tell you in 20 years.' His answer is what I think the importance of collegiate coaching and the collegiate athletic experience is all about. This coach wasn't willing to measure his team based on their one-dimensional ability to win a championship in football. He was measuring his team on the kinds of people they were going *to become*. I think [that's] what the senior letter is. Even though, to some extent, it has a partial review of the athletic contribution, it is always done within the context of [the] woman's evolution as a human being and her contribution at a higher level. The senior letter is almost a mini-summary of what you view [each] young woman's core character to be. The senior letters are my insights into what makes these women extraordinarily special. The letters are absolutely genuine. A lot of what makes the whole thing special is that the young women know they are getting the letter either the morning of — or the night before — the game and they know that while they're on the field warming up, [it's] going to be read in front of their teammates. The motivation to the team is that they aren't just

COACHING WISDOM

"When it's really tough and grueling, you know it's going to pay off, but there are those days where you're just like, 'Ah man, I just don't have it today.' The thing that makes the difference on those days is the person who is coaching you. Deep down we knew that Andrea Hudy had our best interest at heart. She would never blow us off if we had a question; she would always help us find the answer, no matter what time of day it was. She would always take the time and be there for us when we weren't working out. So, knowing that and feeling that when she's there pushing you during a workout, you'll give that much more because you trust her. " — Ben Gordon playing for a good center forward or a good left midfielder, but they are playing for an extraordinary human being, and the idea in that championship game is to send them out winners.

"You are trying to send them out winners because of your respect and affection for them as people, not out of some athletic legacy. You are playing for reasons beyond the game. You are playing for their soul and character, which is deeper than just playing for a championship. I think what's happened over the years is, our kids in the final game have been, in the most positive way, just ruthless and they desire to send their team out with a thank-you. One value I think sports has is it collects every conceivable passion and emotion, including the exciting and dangerous aspects of physical risk. Blood, sweat, and tears — all those wonderfully dramatic elements that are present in a championship weekend. After the game, your relationship with the player completely changes. At first, they don't realize it, but eventually they do. The dynamic changes. You go from this coach-player relationship to this friendship. There's no more power dynamic. Hopefully if the relationship is a good one, it can evolve into a friendship."

Anson Dorrance knows how to affirm his team members. He has a way with words, and he uses them wisely to demonstrate his care and appreciation for the women who give their all to his program. Frosty Westering, a retired head football coach of Pacific Lutheran, also found a unique way to show his appreciation for the men who played their hearts out in each and every game. He developed a tradition called the Afterglow, which you'll read about more as you continue. And not only were the players affirmed through this tradition, the affirmation and inspiration extended to the families and fans of the team.

Frosty provided ample affirmation whenever someone was giving their all. He was a firm believer that the biggest form of competition is against oneself. He encouraged individual team members to strive to be the very best version of themselves, on and off the field. Frosty cared about his players, his staff, and the entire community — and he wanted every single person he knew to affirm each other and celebrate life.

Former athletic director Paul Hoseth explained why, as nice as the Pacific Lutheran team was on the outside, they were so tough inside. "Over the years, we often did not stack up well physically against our opponents, but the kids performed at a very high level because they were not afraid to fail."[1]

CHALK TALK:

X MAKE AN EFFORT TO LEARN NAMES.
FIND CREATIVE WAYS TO REMEMBER NAMES.
ADDRESS PEOPLE BY NAME.

O TAKE A GENUINE INTEREST IN LEARNING ABOUT YOUR TEAM MEMBERS' LIVES OUTSIDE OF SPORTS. ASK QUESTIONS LIKE, "WHAT'S NEW?" AND GENUINELY LISTEN FOR THE ANSWERS. FOLLOW UP.

X BE ACCESSIBLE.
GO ABOVE AND BEYOND YOUR JOB DESCRIPTION.

O GIVE PLENTY OF PUT-UPS. UTILIZE THE POWER OF A HANDWRITTEN NOTE.

X ENCOURAGE YOUR TEAM MEMBERS TO BE THE BEST VERSIONS OF THEMSELVES RATHER THAN COMPARING THEMSELVES TO OTHERS.

Profiles

TONY DUNGY: Making a Connection

During many of his practices with the Indianapolis Colts, it was the highlight of Hunter Smith's day when Head Coach Tony Dungy would walk up to him — as a punter, Smith points out, he did a lot of standing around at practice, waiting and watching — and want to learn more about Smith's Christian worship band, Connersvine.

"He would come up to me and want to talk about writing songs and how I did it," said Smith, a 12-year NFL veteran. "I would find myself lost in this discussion of artistic license and literature as it pertains to writing books and music with Tony during practice. For me it was a band; for others it would be talking to them about their alma mater, or a coach they had in high school and he coached against them. People might say that's not professional, but it's absolutely professional. It's being involved."

The ability Dungy had to be real, to be authentic, set him apart from all the other coaches Don Davis played for during his 11-year NFL career as a linebacker and special teams player with six teams.

"Coach Dungy really taught from a fatherly perspective," Davis says. "You played hard for him because you didn't want to let him down. There was correction, you were held accountable, which you have to have on the football field, but at the same time you were treated like a man, and he had an ability to connect with athletes from that perspective. And I think because of that, he cared. He knew my wife's name. He would ask how my day was going. I think that was his gift. His ability to connect, and because you knew he cared about you as a man, it makes you want to play for him all the more."

Take a moment to think about a teacher or coach in your life who valued you as a person and cared about what you cared about, because if it was important to you, it was important to them. Now, how did you know they cared about you? If you could rewind the mental video footage of your life, there are undoubtedly many key moments where that teacher or that coach was there to do or say just the right thing when you needed it most. And many times, they were simply present, there to listen and engage. They took a sincere, genuine interest in your well-being. As you reflect on this, you may want to write down some of the qualities, words, and actions that define true leadership for you.

TOM OSBORNE: Helping Players Feel Valued

Tom Osborne, retired head coach of the Cornhuskers football team, has had a major influence on his players over his 25-year career. Jim Pillen remembers standing in the shadows of Nebraska's Memorial Stadium one hot August afternoon in 1974, waiting for the third day of freshman football practice to begin. He was still in awe of where he was and what he was doing.

All those Saturdays throughout childhood, he had gathered around the radio with his family to listen to Cornhuskers games. When he was ten years old, he came to this stadium for the first time. He wore his Nebraska red to dutifully contribute to the sea of red that had filled the stadium's brim since Nebraska's consecutive sellout streak began on November 3, 1962, a streak still alive today. Being surrounded by fellow Nebraskans from all over the state, united by one passion, one cause, cemented the dream he held for his future — to play football for the Cornhuskers.

So just three days before that third practice, he traveled the 80 miles southeast from the family farm to report to preseason training camp. Pillen had earned all-state honors as a quarterback and linebacker at Lakeview High in Columbus, Nebraska, and was recruited to play for the Cornhuskers. He followed in the footsteps of his older brother, Clete, who joined the team as a walk-on, non-scholarship player just two years before.

As Pillen stood there waiting for the drills to begin, something happened that still moves him to this day. Head Coach Tom Osborne jogged toward the players waiting to practice on the field and stopped beside him.

"Hi Jim, how you doing?" Osborne asked.

"Good, Coach," Pillen said, and Osborne nodded and started to jog away. Just as he got about ten steps away, Osborne stopped and walked back to Pillen.

"Jim, I see they have you at cornerback," Osborne said, "and I don't think that fits you best, so tell your position coach that we talked and that you need to move to Monster Man (strong safety)."

Pillen was still amazed while recounting the story more than 36 years later.

"First of all, he said my name, and you can't believe how much that meant to me at that time," Pillen says. "Then for him to think of me, the fourth-string right cornerback on the freshman team, and how that wasn't the best fit for me, that's unbelievable. That year, we had about 95 guys on the freshman team and about 140 on the varsity. So Coach Osborne is responsible for all those young men, and he took the time to not only know my name but to say it to me, and also had thought about how I could help the team more in another position."

During his Nebraska career, Pillen went on to earn All-Big Eight Conference first-team honors as a two-year starter at strong safety. And in 2004, he was inducted into the Nebraska Football Hall of Fame.

But what sticks with Pillen most is that brief conversation with Coach Osborne that hot and humid August afternoon in 1974.

"Those were bewildering days for me, coming from a small high school and wondering how I'd fit into the team," Pillen says. "Coach Osborne showed me that he cared about me and valued me. After that day, I'd run through a brick wall for him."

BRAD STEVENS

BRAD STEVENS: Creating a Sense of Family

Brad Stevens's office in historic Hinkle Fieldhouse on the Butler University campus contains more substance than flash, much like the man who occupies the space. Ask Stevens where he keeps his rings, representing his team's achievements within the Horizon League conference and in the NCAA tournament in recent years, and he starts rummaging around the backs of drawers. "Here's the Final Four ring," he says as he opens the box. Nope, it's a conference championship ring. "Maybe this is it," he says as he pulls another black box from a different drawer. Wrong again. "I think I gave them to my wife for safekeeping," he says. "I hope I did, anyway."

Books sit atop the cabinet next to his desk in a neat row, and include titles by Lou Holtz, Tony Dungy, John Wooden, Ken Blanchard, and Stephen Covey. On top of his desk lays the book *The Dash: Making a Difference with Your Life*, by Linda Ellis and Mac Anderson. Like the authors he reads and the coaches he studies, Stevens values the meaningful relationships he has the opportunity to build as the leader of a group of young men who, at 18 to 22 years of age, are at a crucial learning stage in their lives. And he knows that a big part of that process is simply being available. His players need to know that between all the 6:00 a.m. practices, classes, homework, studying, rehabilitation, lifting, running, and traveling, their head coach will be there when they need him. "They know that they can call me and come in any time," Stevens says. "There's no question about it."

Zach Hahn, a guard who was a key contributor and sometime starter on both Butler Final Four teams, heard the message that he wanted to hear during the first team meeting of his freshman year in 2007. "When we first walk in, Coach Stevens says that what matters most is not what you do while you're here," Hahn recalls. "He says, 'I'll know I'm successful if you come back 20 years from now and you're still wanting to come back to visit campus and see us.'"

When Hahn had the flu and missed a practice during his senior season, Stevens called periodically to see if he needed anything. Then he asked a staff member go check on him while the team practiced. "It's not like it's the one time it happens, it's who he *is*," Hahn says. "If it's six in the morning and we tell him that we need to be let into the gym, he's there to let us in. He's ready to go. Knowing he was there if I needed him outside of basketball gave me somebody I could lean on. And that was great in a head coach, because I think that a lot of times, head coaches are hard to get to at big-time programs. They push a lot of that stuff off to the assistant. Brad takes full ownership and responsibility on that. If we just need to call and talk and it's the weekend, and he's with his family, he would take off and talk to us about our situation and help in any way that he could. While he puts family and faith in front of basketball, and he tells us to put those same things along with education before basketball, he's always there for us."

When Butler lost a third straight league game in early February 2011, their record was 14–9 and appeared to be heading down a path that would leave them on the outside of the NCAA tournament field. It wasn't a speech that pulled the team out of the rut. It wasn't the heroics of one player putting the team on his back. It was the bond that can only be formed by caring.

"Coach Stevens creates a sense of family within the team," former Butler forward Matt Howard says. "It's about relationships. If you don't have a team that has those relationships, that want to be around each other when we go through the kind of stretch that we did earlier this year, you don't climb out of that. You stay down and you sink deeper into a hole and people start to fight, and you're going to have that selfishness come out. But if you actually care about each other and you want to make each other better, keep doing what you're doing, keep working hard, and good things are going to happen. I think that was a really important part of our being able to pull together and do what we did this year."

What Butler did after that point in early February was win the next 14 games in a row, a streak that ended when they lost to UConn in the national championship game.

JOHN WOODEN: Inspiring By Example

John Wooden first left his home state of Indiana and headed out to Los Angeles in 1948, but long before that he coached a young man at South Bend Central High who was proud to call his old coach a friend up until the day Wooden passed away in June 2010. Eddie Ehlers knew Wooden before he was the legendary John Wooden that the rest of the country came to know.

It was in the hallways of Central High that Ehlers and Wooden first started building the foundation for what began as a high school teacher and coach trying to help a sophomore achieve his personal best, and later led to their lifelong friendship.

Ehlers's first visit to his old high school comes a decade after it was refurbished and made into Central High Apartments. Wooden also taught English at Central High, and his classroom is now Apartment 219. His old office next door is now filled in with cement. Ehlers likes what they've done to the place. Little has changed to the interior since he first walked these halls more than 60 years before. The hallways are brown, wide, and clean. The lockers that once lined the hallway are walled over now. The boldly stenciled black-lettered signs are still above the old classrooms. Physics was down the hall, the gymnasium around the corner.

Ed Ehlers was The Man at Central High. Coach John Wooden called Ehlers "maybe the most outstanding all-around athlete I have coached." The Central Bears basketball team played in front of sold-out crowds at the local YMCA because the gym at the high school wasn't big enough. They came and they cheered. And Ed Ehlers was the star. He was an All-State selection on Wooden's basketball and baseball teams (Wooden wouldn't let him play football). He went on to star at Purdue University and play professional basketball for the Boston Celtics and professional baseball in the New York Yankees organization, and he turned down an opportunity to play football with the Chicago Bears. At Central High, Ed Ehlers was the guy all his classmates wanted to be. And if they couldn't be him, then at least they could vote for him — he was elected class president all three years at Central.

"Eddie was our hero, our star," says Bernie Peczkowski, the drum major in the Central High band and Ehlers's classmate. "He was the kind of guy you enjoyed being around. He had that magnetism. I mean, it didn't matter what background you came from, Eddie was nice to everyone down the line. I'm proud to say that I voted for him for president all three years."

Those may be the memories of his classmates, but Ed Ehlers has different thoughts as he faces the old office door of his favorite high school teacher. Sure, he was popular, good-looking, and the best athlete in town. But Ehlers knows that without the loving guidance of the man who worked behind this office door, he wouldn't have been anyone's "hero." While Ed was the guy his classmates wanted to be, Ed wanted to be like John Wooden.

During his high school days, Ehlers found any number of reasons to come see Coach Wooden. Ed counts himself blessed that he had other coaches and teachers who cared as much as Wooden. But there was something about Wooden that resonated with Ehlers. Part of it may have been that Wooden was a great athlete himself, a three-time All-American guard at Purdue. Also, Ehlers knew that even if he was the last guy on the bench, Wooden would still care as much. There was something different about Wooden. Something real. When Ed visited Coach Wooden in this office, he knew that he was talking to a man he could learn from. Someone who would always give him the truth, like it or not. Someone who would always be there for him.

The memories are strong and fill Ehlers's head like pictures in a scrapbook as he stands in the hallway.

Once when Ed was visiting Wooden in this office, the superintendent of the school district stopped by. "Where do you think you'll go to college?" the superintendent asked Ehlers. "Aw, I don't know, I've got offers from everywhere," Ed replied with an arrogant tone. The superintendent left and Wooden laid into his pupil.

"Who do you think you are?" Wooden asked. "Don't you ever let me catch you talking to somebody with the attitude you just showed."

Ehlers, embarrassed, slinked out of the office and walked away that day during his senior year in 1941. As he says now, "Here I was thinking I was Charlie Hot Potatoes with all these offers, and Wooden really put me back in my place. I still hear him saying that to me. It's stayed with me ever since — always remain humble and respectful."

A lot of moments that happened here in this office have stuck with Ehlers. Like when Ehlers had an offer from the Boston Red Sox to sign a contract for four times what Ehlers's dad earned as a salesman; it was to this office he came to ask Wooden what he thought. Wooden told him to pass up the money and go to college and get an education, and more money would be waiting

(continued on next page)

after graduation. Wooden was right.

It's not the wins and losses that have stuck with the Ehlers, but the times in between — the times when his coach's concern and care for him and his teammates just seemed to be a given. They didn't realize the true impact of Wooden's sincerity and generosity until years later, like when Ehlers broke his nose during a basketball practice.

"I caught an elbow and it just cracked," Ehlers recalls. "I couldn't breathe and [my nose] was all bent over, and of course after that I was subject to colds because I couldn't breathe. One day, I was home and a doctor knocked on our door and introduced himself. He said, 'I want you to come to the hospital Saturday; I'm going to operate on your nose.'"

Ehlers interrupted the doctor, telling him thank you, but his family didn't have medical insurance and couldn't afford the bill.

"It's already taken care of," the doctor said. "I'll see you this Saturday." Ehlers went to the hospital and had his nose straightened. The doctor never mentioned who arranged the operation. When asked about this some 70 years later, Wooden smiled and said, "I'm really glad that Eddie was able to get that fixed," then quickly changed the subject. But Ehlers knows.

"My folks couldn't afford a doctor to operate on me or anything," Ehlers says. "I know that Wooden was the one behind it. Although he always denied it and never said it, he arranged for it. I thanked him and he just kind of nodded, but never said anything."

It wasn't so much that his old coach always had the right answer when he came up those worn stairs to visit him in his office. It's that Wooden cared.

"People ask me, 'What was so great about John Wooden?'" Ehlers says softly, still standing in front of the dark brown office door. "And as I look back, yes, he was a great coach. He gave great pep talks and great practices. But that's not what I remember.

"What I remember is him as a person. He was so much more than a coach. Coach Wooden was such an example of sincerity and honesty that I wanted to be like him. We weren't just players to him. We were people he cared about. He got within you. And you believed in him."

Ehlers points to the large cream-colored wall across the hallway.

"If he told you to run through that wall, you'd do it because you believed in him."

More than seven decades have passed since Ehlers was officially on Wooden's class roster. But Ehlers remains Wooden's student for life.

ANDREA HUDY: Caring Beyond the Call of Duty

Andrea Hudy has framed NBA jerseys of two of her most prized pupils adorning neighboring walls of her office, overlooking the weight room at the University of Kansas. Emeka Okafor and Ben Gordon are two young men whose minds and bodies Hudy helped strengthen for the rigors of big-time college basketball during their time at the University of Connecticut. They won a national championship together in 2004, the same year Okafor went second overall in the NBA draft, followed by his Huskies teammate, who was taken with the third overall pick in the first round.

Across the room hangs a framed photo of Hudy with the Connecticut women's basketball team at the White House with former President Bush after that team also won the national championship in 2004. Slung over a chair are the signed WNBA jerseys of superstars Sue Bird and Diana Taurasi, both of whom won national championships with Hudy at UConn. There are many more mementos that cover her walls, some of which highlight the eight national championships she was a part of as a strength coach at UConn: five women's basketball, two men's basketball, and one men's soccer. As the Kansas men's basketball strength and conditioning coach since 2004, Hudy added a ninth national championship in 2008.

Ben Gordon had an All-American career at UConn and has had a successful six-year run in the NBA, most recently with the Detroit Pistons. From the time that Hudy first became his strength coach at UConn, Gordon has known that Hudy is there to help. And he still leans on her. When Gordon needed to buy equipment for his home gym a few years ago, he called Hudy. When Gordon needs input on putting a new workout regimen together, he calls Hudy. Gordon is even planning on coming to Kansas to train with Hudy this summer, because he knows it will make him better. That belief started those days in the weight room at UConn.

He says, "She's not the type of person who has the attitude, 'I'm coming to do my job and when my day's over, it's over.' With Hudy, caring doesn't stop at 5:01."

ANSON DORRANCE

ANSON DORRANCE: A Man of Letters

Anson Dorrance, head coach of the North Carolina women's soccer team, knows that character is what makes a true champion.

While a senior in high school in 2006 in Lawrence, New York, Caroline Boneparth fit the profile of a Dorrance player: all-state, National Merit Scholar, valedictorian. Schools across the country offered her soccer and academic scholarships. Wherever she enrolled, she would embrace the academic challenge — that was a given — and maybe even apply for the Rhodes Scholarship. When considering soccer programs, she knew she would probably have a good chance to start or at least earn playing time right away as a freshman at most of the schools.

However, she didn't choose those schools. She chose the University of North Carolina, joining a soccer program that has 728 wins in 798 matches and is led by a head coach who has won the national championship, on average, about every two out of three seasons he's coached.

"I knew I was going against the odds and thought that, best-case scenario, I would work my way into the rotation junior or senior year," Boneparth says. "It's not like I didn't know what I was getting into. I came in my freshman year, as I said, I didn't expect to play, but it still doesn't make it any easier not to. The conversation that I had with Anson at the end of my freshman year was that he wanted me to be a leader on the team. I kind of struggled with that because I didn't think I had the credibility."

She did. During practices, she would outhustle and outmuscle her teammates to the ball, then help them up and tell them that they'd better step it up, because they'd be playing someone better than her in the next match. She would demand her teammates' best effort and be there encouraging them when they doubted if they could do it. Though Boneparth played sparingly during her years at Carolina, her teammates never measured her value in minutes played.

"He would stop practice and call everyone over, and you'd think he was going to talk about the great goal that was just scored," three-time captain Ali Hawkins says. "Instead, he would make a point of saying how great

Caroline's attitude was or how great her leadership was. I think that's pretty incredible, too. One of the things that he does frequently is he makes a point of publicly praising people."

There's a moment that defines Boneparth's collegiate career for Dorrance. It was during the NCAA tournament, and because of rules that place limits on how many players can be on the bench during a match, some players can't suit up and have to sit in the grandstands. One postseason as an underclassman, Boneparth earned a spot to be on the bench, but knew that a senior would have to watch her remaining games from the stands. She wrote an e-mail to Dorrance, asking to give up her spot on the bench so the senior could join the team on the sidelines. Dorrance wrote a letter to Boneparth's dad, telling him how impressed he was with his daughter.

In her senior year, after all the years of practicing hard and not playing much, Boneparth would be part of a team that reached the national championship game again. She had already been a part of two national championships (in 2006 and 2008). This could make it three. But almost bigger than that, she knew she would be getting a senior letter. Only seniors who reach the national championship game receive a letter from Dorrance. Only then, Dorrance explains, because you know that the next game is definitely going to be the last of the career, and therefore it can only be written in that "emotional cauldron." The night before the championship game Dorrance gets his note cards out in his hotel room and writes . . . and writes . . . to each senior, the words tumbling from his heart.

Before that championship match against Stanford on December 6, 2009, Dorrance read the senior letters, including Boneparth's, to the underclassmen in the locker room before the game. Tears flowed freely, as they had before championship games before.

North Carolina beat Stanford 1–0 that day in front of a record-breaking crowd. Boneparth didn't play. But she now had her letter. She had stolen a few moments of alone time before the game to read it, and the rush of emotion helped her cheer her teammates on harder than perhaps she ever had before.

Ali Hawkins says, "I can remember talking to Tobin (Heath, former All-American), and she said, 'It's so stupid how the newspapers pick up on me or Casey [Nogueira, former national player of the year], but they don't even realize the only reason we're winners is because of Caroline Boneparth.' It

(continued on next page)

was so funny, and she was so honest about it when she said it. There was a real sense of indignation in her voice when she was expressing that the world didn't see it. I think a lot of that came from Anson perpetually making sure people thought that way."

Dorrance was sure to always point out what Boneparth brought on the practice field and to the team. To this day, she'll pull the letter out when she needs a pick-me-up. And when she gets it out and opens it, here's what she reads:

Dec. 2009

Dear Caroline,

Here are parts of an e-mail I sent your father in Nov. of 2007 right after you had decided you were going to sacrifice your place on our narrow NCAA roster for a senior. Given how these roster spots are cherished, the gesture gets right to the core of your character and I was so impressed with your selfless spirit. 'Peter, in over 30 years I have coached many extraordinary players but the players I cherish are the extraordinary human beings. They don't number as many. . . . We do run a meritocracy, which is why that place on the NCAA roster was Caroline's to give. There is no one on my current roster that I would love to see fight her way onto the field more than Caroline. I silently cheer for the "human beings" on my roster and I hope somehow as the playing time gets divided up in sometimes excruciatingly painful directions, they don't feel this is any kind of indictment of their real value.'

I am so happy you allowed me to write your Rhodes recommendation. I could see your character early . . . do you remember this note?

'Caroline, . . . we want you to come join us but the risks are always there for anyone that selects this program and we never wanted you to think this would be given to you. There are other places you could go that would be easier with more guarantees . . . I am excited you did not take that path. There will never be anything except challenge about playing soccer for Carolina but the few (like you) that do will have already passed a significant test because they want to see what they are really made of . . . some people never want to know. And here is what I have learned: "Not often in the story of mankind does a (person) arrive on earth who is both steel and velvet, who is as hard as rock and soft as drifting fog, who holds in (her) heart and mind the paradox of terrible storm and peace unspeakable and perfect."

This is you. You are so strong and sweet and I cherish you for it. Thank you for taking "care" of everyone for four wonderful years. I am going to miss you.
—Anson

FROSTY WESTERING: Sharing in the Afterglow

Frosty Westering, retired head football coach of Pacific Lutheran, was a perennial power at the NAIA and Division III levels. His coaching style was so unique that a full-length movie is in the works to chronicle him and his approach. Nothing better captures how he made the team-first concept work than his post-game tradition of Afterglow.

In an age when players celebrate every play with some sort of hot-dog response, that isn't allowed at Pacific Lutheran. On the sidelines before a game, Westering would tell them, "Our opponents come to BEAT us; we come to BE us." When they scored, there were no celebrations, no dancing routines. They would take a respectful knee when a teammate or opponent was injured. That's because their coach always said: "To get respect, you have to give it." They ran onto and off the field holding hands in a human chain. Rather than a collection of individuals, they played as a team.

Such behavior as holding hands didn't mean they backed down from anybody, though. They would help you off the ground and pat you on the back. Then, they would go on and beat the stuffing out of you. One opponent, Grady McGovern of St. John's, had this to say: "When they knock you on your butt, they help you up. They're the classiest team I've ever played against."[2] Paul Hoseth, former athletic director and assistant coach under Westering, explained why, as nice as these teams were on the outside, they were so tough inside. "Over the years, we often did not stack up well physically against our opponents, but the kids performed at a very high level because they were not afraid to fail."[3]

Westering has a saying: "Doing the best is more important than being the best." A good example of that occurred during a high-scoring game. As Westering paced the sidelines, he remarked to a referee, "This is a great game." The official responded, "But, Frosty, you're losing." Westering had this comment after the game was over: "You know, he just didn't understand. Both teams were playing well. You wanted to win, but it didn't matter if you gave it your best shot."[4]

Westering had a unique concept for his players: they were playing

(continued on next page)

for more than just a win. Steve Ridgway, an All-American linebacker in the 1970s, explained a key part of his coach's philosophy. "He believes in developing men who are servant warriors — who find something bigger than themselves to give their lives away to, who are willing to stoop down and kneel and care for the ones who need to be cared for. And then not to stick their chests out and say, 'See what I did? Aren't I great?'"[5]

When the game was over, the team would celebrate and then gather for a round of prayers. After that, they would turn to their fans in the stands. This hour-long "sharing time" became known as the Afterglow, a post-game energizing gathering in which the Lutes met with families and friends. This followed Westering's philosophy: "When in doubt, do the friendly thing."

He used these sessions so that his players could voice their opinions. "I always believed in three or four captains. They would have a meeting every week with all the players. It was a sharing and a feedback time, and then the captains would come to us and say, 'These are some of the things that the guys are thinking, and these are some things that you can adjust yourself.' Because feedback is the breakfast of champions when you know how to use it and so we had a lot of input with players and also one-on-one meetings with the players. We didn't talk about football; we talked about their life and their family and what they wanted to do. Football was kind of at the end. They just felt that we really cared about them, and that makes all the difference in the world."

During the Afterglow, different team members would thank the fans for coming, especially when they were playing on the road. The team discussed the good that came out of that day's game. When away, the Afterglow was held in the bleachers; at home, it was held in the fieldhouse. Westering would moderate, but the show was run by the players, who faced the crowd with bullhorns. Introductions were made and compliments were bandied around. The players would give each other put-ups, which are the opposite of put-downs. They would talk not about winning or losing, but about being together.

Jon Edmonds, an offensive tackle for PLU, has fond memories of the Afterglow sessions. "After the game we would get together," he said. "Players, parents, girlfriends, classmates, and the captains would start off talking about the game. The ups and downs, how it went, and then the captains would bring up certain players that did a fantastic job and they would talk about how they felt. For about an hour we would get together and not necessarily talk about the sport, but talk about the highs and lows of the game."

These group meetings created a powerful bond with their fans. Hoseth pointed out, "How many people can genuinely make a difference in the lives of others? Here, it happened with hundreds or even thousands of people, and it's not just the football players." The point of Afterglow was to embrace everybody. "I've seen middle-aged adults crying when their sons graduate and leave the program, because Frosty has created this environment where even the parents can become really involved in meaningful ways."[6]

During one Afterglow in 1989, John Nelson even found, as he told writer Jon Vaden, a "reason for living."[7] Nellie was a quadriplegic who had arthrogryposis, a rare congenital disorder that locked his joints from the neck down. Nellie felt neglected by his adopted parents, and he often contemplated suicide. While attending PLU, he was invited to attend an Afterglow by a backup quarterback. It followed a team loss, and Nelson was moved by the team's ability to look past the disappointment. Instead of hanging their heads, they regarded the game as a learning experience. They lived up to one of Westering's favorite sayings: "Character: Our best piece of equipment." They sang songs together and ate cookies, handed out by their coach. They gave Attaway cheers to anyone who wanted one, including one for Nelson. "Hey, Nellie! Go, Nellie! Attaway! ATTAWAY!"

He was very moved by their support, and he asked for a turn at the microphone. "You guys have taught me more about life tonight than anybody ever has," he said. "After coming to the game and this Afterglow and seeing the friendliness of you people, I'm going to become the number one fan of PLU football." The next Tuesday, Westering met up with Nellie and invited him to attend a practice. He gave him a jersey with the number 39. Nellie was soon attending practice every day. He became a member of Westering's staff, helping freshmen get used to college life. He said that he considered Westering his inspiration. "He's someone who has changed my life," he said. "I would do anything for him."[8]

Nellie passed away in 2009 at the age of 44. Speaking during the funeral gathering, Westering led the gathering in an emotional Attaway cheer.

"[Nellie] liked the Attaway Cheer. And he liked Go Lutes," said Westering. "So we're going to do a Go Lutes and an Attaway."

Then he held up a #39 jersey with "NELLIE" on the front, and through his tears he said, "Nellie, you're in the game." He ended by placing the jersey over the casket.

His son Scott, who was his offensive coordinator for 20 years, said after they won their last championship in 1999, "My father has never focused on winning, and yet he is one of the winningest coaches that ever coached the game of football. His teams never started a season by setting a goal to win the national championship, to go undefeated — or for that matter, to win our conference. That's so contrary with what's out there in the world."[9]

No pressure. Go out there and play for your teammates. That's the kind of football coach everyone wishes they'd played for. Frosty Westering wasn't just teaching his students how to win on the gridiron, he was teaching them how to win in life. Former player Steve Ridgway summed up what he learned: "His legacy will be the young men who are good fathers, and men of integrity in the marketplace, and great husbands, and people who contribute back to society more than what society will give to them," he said. "They'll be servants."[10]

As everyone did during his long and storied career, it's best to let Westering have the last word. As he so often told his players, "The real measure of me is not what I can do compared to others, but what I can do compared to my best self."

Chapter 2

COMMUNICATING EFFECTIVELY

"COMMUNICATION WORKS FOR THOSE WHO WORK AT IT."
— JOHN POWELL

Do you remember the game of "telephone" — that childhood activity in which a message starts off one way and is whispered through a long chain of people, and by the time the last person hears the message, it's something completely different? Messages are often misconstrued, not only in sports but in all avenues of life. We tend to view the world through our own set of lenses, and we assume others are wearing the same lenses we have on. This is not the case. You are surrounded by people who think, act, and communicate differently than you do. What does this ultimately mean? In short, if you are in charge of a group of people, whether in sports, business, or any other arena of life, you are going to have to pay attention to how you communicate with others, in order to send and receive messages as effectively as possible.

Understand your own communication style and be yourself. At the same time, know your personnel. Team surveys, personality assessments, and one-on-one conversations are incredibly helpful options for gathering information about how your team members communicate best. Some people want data — if you show them the numbers, they will understand where you're coming from. Others want encouragement — you need to give them a pat on the back before you supply the necessary constructive feedback. Learning about and truly appreciating these differences will give you an edge — you will be able to communicate as effectively as possible with your team members.

One thing that rings true across all communication styles is this: direct and honest communication is highly appreciated. People feel respected when you give it to them straight. Especially when it comes to defining roles on your team. A wonderful illustration of this comes from Brad Stevens, the Butler coach who led his men's basketball program to two straight Final Fours in 2010 and 2011. Players who went from starting positions to coming off the bench were able to

COACHING WISDOM

"It means a lot that Coach Stevens took the time to talk to me about going from a starter to coming off the bench. When someone does that, you know you are valued. It's like when you walk into work one day and you have a note on your desk that you aren't in the same position you used to be in or you walk into practice and the lineup is changed without any kind of discussion. You're like, *Well, does my boss or coach really care about me?* You don't mean this in a selfish way where it's all about you, but you do want to be valued. Everyone wants that. Talking is one way that ensures that he values you. To look you right in the face and say, 'Look, this is what we're doing, and this is what I think. I think this is the best thing, and if it's not, then we can change it, but I think it will be.' For him to do that, it means a lot — to me and a lot to other guys as well." — Ronald Nored, Butler basketball accept and excel in their new roles, thanks to Stevens's ability to communicate the change to them respectfully and to sell them on the purpose for the switch.

"THE TWO WORDS 'INFORMATION' AND 'COMMUNICATION' ARE OFTEN USED INTERCHANGEABLY, BUT THEY SIGNIFY QUITE DIFFERENT THINGS. INFORMATION IS GIVING OUT; COMMUNICATION IS GETTING THROUGH."
— SYDNEY J. HARRIS

Butler's Brad Stevens emphasizes the importance of having one-on-one conversations in order to build trust and motivate people. His student-athletes express their strong belief in his integrity, which is partly based on the fact that they feel respected by his effort to invite them into his thought process when making decisions that affect them. Whether you're a coach, teacher, business leader, or parent, if you are communicating news that might be unpopular to the receiver of the message, it's important for you to provide a rationale for why you've made the decision you have. It is far easier for people to get on board with a difficult decision or a tough critique if they understand where it's coming from. Share your reasoning. National Hockey League coaching legend Scotty Bowman changed his approach to players in the latter half of his career to do just that. He became a more open person, according to former NHL goalie Tom Barrasso, who played for Bowman during the Pittsburgh Penguins' championship run for the 1992 Stanley Cup. Bowman placed importance on adapting to the changing needs of his players, and when he noticed players wanting more feedback, he made greater efforts to communicate with them, particularly regarding changes in playing time.

Frankly, some conversations are going to be uncomfortable. Think back to the last time you had to have a tough conversation with someone. What was the topic? How did it go? Could you have handled it more effectively? The fact that you handled it at all is a good start. The decision to communicate is the first step. Often, people assume that someone understands their expectations or should know how they feel. We cannot expect others to read our minds. Tell your team members what you're thinking and what the plan is if it affects them. Be real with them.

Be respectful when you share constructive feedback with your team members. Criticize the performance, not the performer. Be specific about what you've noticed. Be clear about your expectations for behavioral change, and do your best to convey the belief that this change is possible. Former Notre Dame football coach Lou Holtz believed in this philosophy wholeheartedly.

Dick Gould, retired Stanford tennis coach, used a variety of communication methods — verbal and nonverbal, tough and humorous — to bring out the best in his team members, to intimidate their opponents, and to sell recruits on the program.

> ## "THE MOST IMPORTANT THING IN COACHING IS TO CRITICIZE THE PERFORMANCE, NEVER THE PERFORMER."
> — LOU HOLTZ

You are a good listener if your team members feel heard by you. So how do you know if someone thinks you understand what they're trying to say to you? Here's a piece of advice that may sound silly, but it works: just reflect back to them what you heard them saying. For example, "So, what I'm hearing you say is that

COACHING WISDOM

"[H]e had a way of saying, 'Gotta get better for tomorrow.' He never belittled anybody, not once. He would point out that we have to get better in this area or we have to do this better, but it was never, 'Johnny, this was an awful play, and this is the worst I've ever seen.' You never heard anything like that. I think that's why guys loved playing for him."

— Don Davis, Former NFL linebacker, on Tony Dungy, his head coach with the Tampa Bay Buccaneers you're not feeling confident about this change in position." Paraphrase their message. Then follow up with, "Is that right?" or something of that nature, to ask for clarification as to whether you truly understood. This does not mean that you have to agree with them. It simply means that you are acknowledging their position. You are giving credence to their perspective. Of course, since you're in charge, you get to make the call. Ultimately, your decision may or may not line up with what your team member wants. However, even when individuals are disappointed by the outcome of conversations with you, it will be much easier for them to digest difficult news when they feel truly heard by you.

This is easiest when you genuinely care. Direct communication in the context of a caring relationship is a powerful thing, as evidenced by former Nebraska football coach Tom Osborne's coaching style.

> ## "THE MOST BASIC OF ALL HUMAN NEEDS IS THE NEED TO UNDERSTAND AND BE UNDERSTOOD. THE BEST WAY TO UNDERSTAND PEOPLE IS TO LISTEN TO THEM."
> ## — DR. RALPH NICHOLS

Championship coaches like Osborne know how to empower others to strive to reach their full potential. Osborne gifted his team members with a voice. Think about this for a moment: when you are designated as the person in charge, you are imbued with power. You can certainly make communication a one-way street when you're the boss, but people are likely to feel minimized and to rebel in response to that approach. Instead, consider taking a page from Osborne's book. Approach communication with the mentality that you are "giving away" some of your power to the people reporting to you. Sound crazy? Maybe it is a little crazy, but it works. Most people like to have an opportunity to share their opinion.

People relish having a voice that's valued. And perhaps the most important outcome of the empowerment approach is this: when people contribute to the game plan, they are going to be more apt to buy into the system. When your team members are given an opportunity to communicate with you in order to help shape the team's activities and goals, they are going to be on board. And later, if team members somehow detract from the team's efforts, you can remind them that they were a part of orchestrating the plan. Another benefit of giving your team a voice is that then your team members can hold each other accountable. When they have all helped determine the path to success, and one person deviates, team members will feel a sense of ownership and will be more likely to call out those who are getting in the way of that success. Empowerment. It's a simple concept, but so many leaders do not implement it. Consider for a moment a few simple methods for including your team in decisions. How can you empower your team? Give them a voice, and they will work that much harder.

Sometimes, as we've said, information can be difficult to share. At times, news may be tough to receive. But during the course of my interviews with coaches for this book, many of them emphasized two things regarding communication: people want to feel heard, and they appreciate honesty. Be authentic when you communicate with others. While directness can be uncomfortable, your team members will respect you for valuing them enough to be real and up-front with them.

CHALK TALK:

X UNDERSTAND YOUR OWN COMMUNICATION STYLE AND BE YOURSELF. GATHER INFORMATION ABOUT HOW INDIVIDUALS ON YOUR TEAM COMMUNICATE BEST.

O BE DIRECT AND BE HONEST. PROVIDE A RATIONALE FOR YOUR DECISIONS. BE AS OPEN AND FORTHRIGHT AS THE SITUATION ALLOWS, ESPECIALLY WHEN DECISIONS MAY BE TOUGH FOR YOUR TEAM MEMBERS TO HEAR.

X ALWAYS BE RESPECTFUL. AVOID BELITTLING OR PUBLICLY SHAMING TEAM MEMBERS. CRITICIZE THE PERFORMANCE, NOT THE PERFORMER.

O TAKE THE TIME TO LISTEN. ASK FOR CLARIFICATION, TO BE SURE YOU'RE TRULY HEARING WHAT THEY ARE SAYING.

X EMPOWER YOUR TEAM BY GIVING THEM A VOICE. INVITE TEAM MEMBERS TO CONTRIBUTE IDEAS. THIS WILL HELP THEM BUY INTO YOUR SYSTEM.

Profiles

SCOTTY BOWMAN: Focusing on Attitude

Scotty Bowman, now 78 years old and having coached his last game in the National Hockey League in 2002 — a Stanley Cup championship win — still gets that feeling of wanting to be close to the ice while sitting in the warmth of his Sarasota, Florida, home during the NHL hockey season.

"I miss everything about coaching," says Bowman, who serves as a senior advisor to the Chicago Blackhawks, for which his son Stan is the general manager. "I enjoyed all parts of the coaching, but the game situations were really enjoyable. Even now at my age — I haven't coached in nine years — during the winter months in the evenings between seven and eight, I still get that feeling that I would like to be behind the bench coaching a game. I coached for a long time, from '56 to '02, and I only missed three or five seasons. I was a coach in the NHL for about 27 years, but I also coached another ten years or 12 years in other leagues. You never lose that aspect at night. I coached so many games that I have a special feeling for the coaches, because I watch their decisions, their moves. It's changed a lot. I had to keep up with the times. I was able to coach in five different decades. I think you have to be able to change. If you don't try things, you never know if they'll work. I always had that philosophy. Not everything is going to work all the time, but some of it will work some of the time, and that's a big asset."

For Bowman, his approach as a coach worked most of the time, to say the least. After entering the NHL as a head coach in 1967, Bowman won a total of nine Stanley Cup championships, leading three different franchises to the Cup — five victories with the Montreal Canadiens, one

(continued on next page)

with the Pittsburgh Penguins, and three with the Detroit Red Wings. Bowman finished his career with a staggering 1,244 wins, the most all-time wins of any coach in NHL history — 462 more than Al Arbour, who is second on the list.

Bowman says he got his work ethic from his father, John, who never took a sick day from his job working for the railroad. He got his competitiveness from his mother, Jane, who he still remembers telling him, "If you like the game, why lose?" Simple enough, Bowman thought, as he set out on a course that has now entrenched him amongst the all-time greatest coaches in any sport.

Earlier in his career, all interactions with his players, and everything he said to the team, were geared toward one thing and one thing only — winning. Over time, however, Bowman wasn't afraid to change, and he did alter his approach. While he wasn't necessarily warm, he did become much more engaged with his players.

"During the last ten to 15 years of my coaching career, I noticed that players were becoming a lot more sensitive," Bowman says. "I found that instead of just pulling a guy off the ice and not talking to him, I needed to take some time to explain *why* I made the change, whether it had to do with his effort or his missing a play or whatever. Earlier in my career, I would have never done that. If they didn't like it, deal with it. But I learned that [the feedback] became critical. As I saw the players' personalities change, I changed."

Tom Barrasso, a NHL Hall of Fame goalie, played for Bowman with the Buffalo Sabres in the 1980s, then again for Bowman with the Pittsburgh Penguins during their 1991–92 Stanley Cup–winning season. At that time, he said:

"Scotty's underlying persona hasn't changed. He still wants to be the best coach in the game. He's still the same in the locker room and the best bench coach ever. It's almost unthinkable that he would have the wrong players on the ice at the wrong time. What has changed tremendously is his mental approach to players. In the past, you could walk right by him and it was like you weren't there. It was impossible to show any friendliness toward him. Now, he might speak to you about your family or the weather. He's a more open person."[1]

Bowman believes the change in his approach with his players was a major factor in his teams winning four Stanley Cups in his final decade of coaching — after the Penguins win, three more with the Detroit Red Wings.

"As a coach, there is a professional part of the job, and there's also a personal part," Bowman says. "That's the most difficult part for people to separate, because you have to make some professional decisions and you have to have some personal interest as well about the person you're dealing with. That's something I always try to keep in mind when I make a tough decision. Whether it's about playing time or signing or releasing a player, it's not a personal decision as much as a professional decision. That's the tough part about dealing with people you have respect for, because there are just tough decisions that have to be made. The singlemost important aspect I ever tried to find out was if a player had a good attitude. As a coach, it wasn't that I put things on a friend basis. There are some coaches who do a better job because that's their personality. I don't think you can change your own personality. You have to always be you and try to keep it all in perspective. I wasn't afraid to change, and I think that's when you become a bit of an innovator."

Sometimes, we fail to communicate at all. This happens for a variety of reasons, including a desire to avoid conflict, difficulty fitting in the time to have the conversation, faulty assumptions that others already know what we want, a belief that others don't need the information, uncertainty about what message we want to send, concern about how the message will be received, or fear of being misunderstood. A breakdown in communication can have a wide range of unwelcome consequences — angry or hurt feelings, strained or broken relationships, reduced confidence, lack of trust, ineffective team work, and performance gaffes that could be costly.

BRAD STEVENS: Establishing Trust

Brad Stevens built the foundation of trust, which exemplifies Butler's basketball program, through many conversations with his players in his office. During an early season slump in the team's first run to the national championship game in 2010, Stevens asked Gordon Hayward to come by his office.

Stevens recognized that, as the most talented player on the team, Hayward's body language, effort, and demeanor would help set the positive tone for his teammates that Stevens knew was needed to get the team out of the funk they were in.

"I think one of the great memories from [the 2009–10 season] is we were 8–4 and struggling," Stevens says, sitting behind his office desk. "I remember Gordon Hayward sat down here and I asked, 'Do you agree with everything we've done every single day? No. Do I think that you're doing everything right? No. But do we agree that we can get a lot accomplished together if, regardless of circumstance, we are completely united? Yes. Do you understand how important it is for you to show that all of the time, because of who will follow? You don't have to say a word as a leader. All you have to do is be all-in.' Those are the kinds of things I think are so important to winning."

Hayward remembers that conversation, too. "It was at a time when our team could have really fallen apart," he says. Hayward, now a member of the Utah Jazz after being drafted in the first round following his sophomore year at Butler in 2010, continues, "Coach called me in and just was very direct, and we had a conversation about how important it was that I be the example of what our team is about — working hard and working together. I've always led by example, and him telling me that helped me understand what he needed from me at that time for our team to be successful."

The team went on a 25-game winning streak after Hayward's conversation with Stevens in his office, the next loss coming to Duke in the championship game, which ended with Hayward's half-court, potentially game-winning shot banking off the backboard and rattling off the rim.

The conversations have not always been as easy to have. Two players, who had key roles during both seasons that ended in the NCAA championship game, had to deal with going from starter to substitute.

Ronald Nored had started at guard in all but five games during his freshman and sophomore seasons, earning the Horizon League Co-Defensive Player of the Year after his sophomore season. Nored started his junior season in 2010–11, up until he suffered a cut on his hand in a February game vs. Youngstown State. Injury aside, Stevens had decided the team would be more successful with Nored coming off the bench, because the starters and the second unit were both playing well.

"That was hard, because he [Nored] had gotten a lot of attention as a starter in the National Championship game, but he wants to be a coach," Stevens says. "I brought him in and said, 'One of the things that this experience needs to prepare you for is your life. If you want to be a coach, this is the best thing you could ever go through.' I told him that we need a second-unit leader. He came off the bench, and I think that was a big deal for us.

"Whether he thought that was my excuse or not, I don't know, but he bought in and he did it. He still played a ton, but I do think he's going to be able to look back on that when he's a coach and know that he's done that. It means more when he's sitting in my chair ten or 15 years from now, and he's looking at a guy, saying, 'I need you to do this. Listen, I've done it. Here's the result.'"

While it was hard being demoted, Nored appreciated and valued his coach being direct with him.

"It was tough to take at first; I'm human, and I had started a lot of games since I had gotten here," Nored says. "But I realized it wasn't personal, and it was something I understood that made our team better. Coach Stevens and I sat down and had a pretty in-depth conversation about the changes that were going to happen. He assured me that it was for the team and for our success, and there was nothing else behind it. If that's the goal, then I'm all for it, and I think things would have been different if we kept our lineups and the things we did. I trusted him when he was starting me, and I trusted him after he made the change. I trust him more than most people in this world, and I think the change was good. I know he always has our team's best interest in mind, and I always have our team's best interest in mind. We're always on the same page in that area. The decisions he makes are the decisions I think are right, and I could never be upset or complain or not agree with any of those because I trust him 100 percent. He's been successful and I've experienced success with him, so I know exactly what he's doing. [Making the change] just shows how smart and intelligent and in tune to the game Coach Stevens really is."

(continued on next page)

Butler, with Nored playing the role of second-unit leader off the bench, reeled off 14 straight victories, a streak that ended in the NCAA championship game loss to Connecticut.

Nored, who coached a 17-and-under AAU basketball team during the summer of 2011 before his senior year at Butler, would like to coach at the college level after his playing career at Butler is completed. And he believes he's had the best role model around.

"It means a lot that Coach Stevens took the time to talk to me about going from a starter to coming off the bench. When someone does that, you know you are valued," Nored says. "It's like when you walk into work one day and you have a note on your desk that you aren't in the same position you used to be in, or you walk into practice and the lineup is changed without any kind of discussion. You're like, well, does my boss or coach really care about me? You don't mean this in a selfish way where it's all about you, but you do want to be valued. Everyone wants that. Talking is one way that ensures that he values you. To look you right in the face and say, 'Look, this is what we're doing and this is what I think. I think this is the best thing, and if it's not then we can change it, but I think it will be.' For him to do that, it means a lot — to me and to many other guys as well. It makes playing for a guy like that a lot easier, because you know he's not out to get you. You're all on the same page. You're not questioning what's going on. You're in a new position. It's something you need to deal with and move on and do the best in the new position you are in. When you do that and have that kind of mentality, it makes it all easy.

"He's had an unbelievable impact on me, and he's part of the reason I want to get into coaching. A lot of people joke, 'Oh, you want to get into this business, there's a lot of stuff you don't see as a player.' You hear some stuff about coaches who don't do things the right way or who make a mistake every now and then and it ends up getting them in trouble, but I can see that it doesn't have to be that way, because I get to see Coach Stevens operate every day. I know that I can still have the integrity that I have right now and still operate at the high level that he does. More important, he's a great husband and father. Those are the three areas that I'm looking forward to eventually. To see he can do that and to watch him in those areas is really cool. And his knowledge for the game of basketball is so rich; he just knows what he's doing all the time. His confidence and the way he inspires his players inspires me just to want to be better, and especially not to let any of my teammates down, because that is most important. As a coach, I want to have a hand in that, and I want to have an impact like he's had on me. That's important to me and something I really look forward to."

Nored's teammate, Zach Hahn, had a similar situation during the 2010–11 season as well. Hahn had earned a starting role at guard early that season, his senior year. Stevens, who pores over statistics to analyze and identify any potential edge for his team, noticed something about Hahn's shooting. He then called Hahn to have a conversation in his office to discuss his findings.

"Zach was 9-for-40 from three-point range as a starter because he's on everybody's scouting report," Stevens says. "He shot 45 percent from three off the bench. He has to come off the bench. There are no ifs, ands, or buts. *He has to come off the bench.* He and [guard] Chase Stigall are pretty similar, so why bring those two off the bench together when you can put Chase in the starting lineup, bring Hahn in later, and then you have a rotation. That was the dynamic that we decided to go with.

"I knew it would be tough for Zach, but I knew he'd understand. I just asked him, 'Numbers-wise, does this make sense to you? Do you like to shoot open shots or contested shots?' He said open shots, so we brought him off the bench. Sometimes, with the ego, starting is more important than anything. But he's got no ego in it, and our guys are great about that."

Maybe Hahn doesn't have any ego, but it still wasn't easy for him.

"Coach Stevens made it a point to always have meetings with us," Hahn says. "Whether it was the beginning of the season, in the summer, right after the season, in the middle of the season, whether we're winning, whether we're losing, he would call in players all the time and talk to them. It wouldn't be about basketball all the time. It would be about their families, or how school's going, or how can he help us succeed in the classroom.

"So when it comes to having a tough conversation, it's not as big a deal because we already have that relationship. When it comes to the basketball court, he's a man of Xs and Os and really getting into statistics and into numbers and looking at how things work offensively as well as the defensive positions. When he looks at those, he looks at patterns and ways we can be more successful on the court, and how one player is more successful in a situation than another. And he really breaks it down into such specifics . . . it's unbelievable what he does."

Hahn continues, "So, for our meeting about me coming off the bench, he

(continued on next page)

was very open about asking, 'What do think about this?' It's more like sitting down with a father figure, because you look up to him and respect him so much and know that he's so knowledgeable about the game. He's not going to tell you anything that's going to hurt you or hurt the team, and he will help you any way he can. If he thinks it would be better for me to come off the bench and my percentages show that, obviously that is where he wants me to be, and that's where he thinks I'd want to be, too. During our meeting, he just said, 'You know, we've looked at the numbers, and you've really shot a lot better coming off the bench, so we think we want you to come off the bench where you can come in and catch people off guard and make two or three (points).'

"That's the kind of way he turns a negative into a positive. And really it *is* a positive the whole time, and you trust that he has figured it out and it's what's best for the team."

When it comes to basketball, what's best for the team is at the heart of every conversation Stevens has in his office.

"One of the things I always tell them is, 'Listen, at the end of the day, we're paid to win — period, end of story,'" Stevens says. "Whoever we think is going to put our team in a position to be successful is going to play. It's nothing personal. The people who are going to help us win, play. You have to put yourself in the best position to do the things necessary that will lead to winning.

"Telling one of our guys that he's no longer going to start is not how I like to have a conversation, but that's the bottom line. I've learned over time that true coaching is one-on-one. I don't think it comes in the five-on-five setting quite as much. The Xs and Os, the adjustments, the things that you do on the court — there's a lot that goes on, but you have to get into the guys. If they're going to give you everything they have, you need to know what makes each of them tick, and they need to know exactly where they stand."

TONY DUNGY: Being Authentic

Tony Dungy (with Peyton Manning and Gary Brackett in photo at left) made an impact on two-time Super Bowl champion Don Davis. Davis's favorite memory of his former head coach wasn't during a game or a locker room speech. It happened on a practice field in Tampa Bay in the late 1990s, while the team was stretching and Dungy was walking nearby.

"One day we were all out at practice stretching, and just like (Dungy) always does, he was walking through the stretch lines talking to players and having conversations, and a few of us were in the back talking about the Powerball lotto," says Davis, now leaning forward as his face starts to light up with a smile. "[The Powerball] was some ungodly amount, like $300 million or something crazy. We were all talking about what we would do with the money. And it was right around the time that Gunther Cunningham [then a Kansas City Chiefs coach] had come out with a statement that he wanted to die on the football field. That's how much he loved it and how long he wanted to coach. He said he loved it so much that he wanted to die on the football field.

"We were joking about the lotto, and we said, 'Coach, do you want to die on the football field? If you won the lotto, would you still coach?' In only the way that he could, he turned and said, 'Men, I love you guys, but I wouldn't even think about it and wouldn't even say good-bye.'

"We all just fell out laughing. That was just real. We knew he didn't play the lotto. He didn't have to preach and say, 'Now, you shouldn't play the lotto,' or anything because we knew where he'd be on that. It was just real and so cool."

More than a decade later, Dungy remembers the moment.

"I remember that," says Dungy, laughing. "I made the point that as much as I love this, it's not life and death. It's not the end of the world. I have a lot of things I want to do besides die on this football field."

The ability Dungy had to be authentic set him apart from all the other

(continued on next page)

coaches Davis played for during his time with six different teams in his 11-year NFL career. Davis believed that he could approach and speak with his coach about anything because he would be available. He knew Dungy would listen and be honest.

"It was always an open-door policy; you could go in any time to his office, or he'd always be walking the halls," says Davis, who is now a regional director with the NFL Players Association. "Coach Dungy was always around, and some coaches [I've had] aren't around that much. He would stop and talk to you and see how you were doing. He would take time to point out something you might have done well on the field or if you didn't do something so well. Then he had a way of saying, 'Gotta get better for tomorrow.' He never belittled anybody, not once. He would point out that we have to get better in this area or we have to do this better, but it was never, 'Johnny, this was an awful play, and this is the worst I've ever seen.' You never heard anything like that. I think that's why guys loved playing for him."

Davis recalls an instance where he was injured in the middle of the season in Tampa Bay, and the team needed to make some roster moves, resulting in Davis being released for a short time. The young player was not very well versed on the NFL rules regarding such matters.

"I had gotten hurt and I wasn't going to play that week, so Coach Dungy brought me in to his office to explain to me that I was going to come on the trip and I was going to travel with the team, even though I wasn't going to play," Davis says. "He told me that because of numbers, we needed another fullback or something on offense, so they were actually going to release me before the night. Which means I would go through waivers, but they were going to pick me right back up on Monday if I cleared waivers [no other NFL team claimed him]. Coach Dungy explained to me exactly what was going to happen — that is so rare in the NFL. Normally, that would have been the general manager or somebody on that level, but he handled it personally, and I loved that. When Monday came, I went over there and it went just like he said it would. To have that one-on-one conversation and a personal guarantee of how things would happen meant a lot. I was still young in the league at that time and I didn't even know you could do things like that, but for him to take the time and explain it and walk me through it made a big impression on me."

Davis believes the accessibility and honesty of Dungy is why his players loved him and played hard for him. Even during games, in the heat of competition, Dungy remained the same person. One game in particular stands out to Davis.

"We weren't playing very well against Green Bay, and it was really one we needed to win in order to secure a better placement in the playoffs," Davis says. "Guys were upset, and you could see the frustration in [Dungy]. He called the defense together and said, 'Listen, we need you to make this play. We're down right now and things look bleak, but all we got is us, and if we're going to win it's going to come down to you all.'

"Now, we didn't end up winning, but the fact was he could have been screaming and kicking, but instead he said, 'Hey, we can't do anything about the game so far. We haven't played well, but we still have a chance to win — that's the good news. We need you to make a play. So who's going to do it?' That was powerful, because we wanted to do it — for us and for him. We didn't end up winning, but the way he spoke to us in that situation really captures him as a coach. He was with us, wanting to help us get it done. He was always with us, never against us."

People value honesty. Your team members will appreciate you being direct with them, just as Dungy was direct with Davis. Dungy also paid attention to the manner in which he delivered messages to his team. As Davis points out, Dungy was always respectful, never belittling or humiliating anyone. This is the next crucial step in effective communication — the delivery of the message. It is important to choose the right place and time to have a conversation. Delivering a tough message to a team member in front of others, with the intention of causing shame or embarrassment, is ultimately not going to work well. It may lead to an initial spike in performance if the person is driven to prove you wrong, but feedback designed to embarrass can severely damage trust. Furthermore, this type of public shaming can lead the individual to spiral downward in confidence and performance, to feel reluctant to buy into the program, to discontinue participation, or even to deliberately sabotage success.

LOU HOLTZ: Three Rules to Remember

Lou Holtz knew that Marcus Thorne was one of the smartest men on the team — heck, even the school. But for some reason, he couldn't get the plays right. As a walk-on, Thorne had just switched from linebacker to fullback, a position he had never played before. During those practices at Notre Dame in the mid-90s, he would always go full speed, and only sometimes would it be in the right direction.

Thorne, now an orthopedic surgeon, laughs at those days on the practice field. "I'd be so determined to make an impact, an impression, that I would be going all out all the time, and I'd sometimes forget the specifics of the play," Thorne says. "I'd make an impression, but not the one I wanted to. And I can still see Coach Holtz walking up to me on the field to correct me."

Holtz says, "He's a good doctor now, a great guy, a good football player, but as a fullback he always went the wrong way. I'd stop practice and say, 'Marcus Thorne, someday I'm going to be retired and I'm going to pick up the newspaper, and I'm going to read that Dr. Thorne cut off the wrong leg. I'm going to have to put a stick in your hand, and we're going to have to call the plays to the stick and away from the stick.'"

Holtz smiles at the memory. Then he pauses before making a serious point.

"Let me tell you the most important thing in coaching — criticize the performance, never the performer," Holtz says.

Thorne would eventually get the plays right more often than not, making enough of a positive impression to earn a starting position and a full scholarship as a senior. Thorne laughs as the realization hits him that he still quotes his football coach from his playing days at Notre Dame, back in the early to mid-90s. Whether he's with his four kids or with his team in the operating room, Thorne finds himself quoting Holtz.

"There are times when we're in the operating room, and something doesn't quite go as planned," Thorne says. "And I'll say to our team, 'Things are never as bad as they seem, and things are never as good as they seem — the reality is somewhere in between.' It seems to calm everybody down; it certainly calms me down and helps me focus. That's something Coach Holtz would say to us all the time, during practice, during games, when were struggling, and when we were on top.

"Coach Holtz always had a way to correct us that was fun and never about our worth as a person, but about the action we took. That's a big part of how I am today, how I lead my family and my team at work."

Holtz says, "Three rules — do what's right, do your very best, treat others like you'd like to be treated — enable you to criticize the performance, never the performer. You say, 'Jim, you're an All-American. I know damn well that's not the best you can do.' I used three words of profanity when coaching. I used 'damn,' 'hell,' and 'ass.' They're all in the Bible. I'd say, 'I know that's not the best you can give, and I want to know why. I'm giving you the best. These guys are giving you the best. If you want to fail, then you have the right to fail. You do not have the right to cause other people to fail because you don't fulfill your obligation.' I didn't attack them. I attacked the performance, and that's critical. When people need love and understanding the most is usually when they deserve it the least. That is true with children. It is true with coaches and with players. You have to make sure you remember that."

Holtz understood how important it was to direct his criticism towards the person's actions, rather than labeling the person. And by taking that approach, he ensured a greater likelihood that his team members would trust him, buy into his program, maintain their confidence, and believe in their ability to make improvements in the future.

Coach Lou Holtz's players also appreciated his sense of humor, which allowed him to soften the manner in which he provided feedback, without dulling the message. Pay special attention to your nonverbal communication, particularly your body language, and be mindful of the tone of voice you use when you speak. "Try it again — you can do better" could be taken as encouragement if delivered with the right tone and energy, or it could be received as demeaning and discouraging if accompanied by a big sigh and an eye roll. When you are in charge of a group of people, like it or not, most of them will look to you for approval. Your words and your mannerisms can convey a broad host of messages, and it's a safe bet that your team members will spend extra energy trying to analyze and reanalyze what you meant when you looked at them a certain way or what you were thinking when you did not give them any feedback. While you can't prevent all miscommunications from occurring, you can do your part to minimize them by being mindful of your verbal and nonverbal communication, and by making an effort to be sincere, direct, and clear about how your message is designed to help the team perform at an optimal level.

TOM OSBORNE: Teaching How to Deal with Adversity

Tom Osborne, Nebraska's head football coach, was paying attention to Steve Taylor. Fresh off of a five-touchdown-passing performance against UCLA just two days before, Taylor was feeling great about his second start as the quarterback at Nebraska. The five touchdown passes set a new school record. The victory, in just the second game of the 1987 season, came for a Nebraska program that usually featured their traditional run-first approach on offense and propelled his team up the national polls.

Taylor was beginning his junior season, his first season as the starting quarterback, and he was riding high on his record-setting performance.

"I'll never forget it, that Monday after the UCLA game, we walked out of our quarterbacks meeting," Taylor says, "and Coach Osborne pulled me aside, and he said, 'Just remember, when things are going great, the quarterback is the hero. They get all the glory. They get too much. When things are going bad, the quarterback gets all the blame.' When Coach Osborne said that, it really helped bring me back down to what was important."

The message stuck with Taylor eight weeks later when his team, then ranked number one in the national polls, lost a hard-fought game to Big 8 Conference rival Oklahoma 17–7.

"We were number one, and that was a huge loss," Taylor says. "But Coach Osborne said, 'Just keep doing what you're doing. You're going to come back and have better days.' It's that kind of advice that has stuck with me to this day. You want to win. Winning is very, very important. You want to do your best, but there's also more to life than winning a football game. That taught me how to deal with adversity. When things don't quite go your way for one reason or another, just keep your head up, do what you're doing, and eventually you're going to succeed. That's what happens. I've won some really big games, and we lost some really big games. I learned the most from the games we lost. You remember the wins and the great wins, but you remember the losses and you learn from them. The perspective Coach shared of just staying the course and working hard is something I always kept in the back of my mind. You don't want to take too much credit for yourself. Obviously, it's the team. Some players can get big-headed. He had a great ability to help us keep everything in perspective."

Osborne's honest approach is what attracted Taylor to Nebraska as a top recruit out of San Diego's Lincoln High School. After a senior season, his only at Lincoln High after moving from Fresno (California), in which he broke former Lincoln High star and now NFL Hall of Famer Marcus Allen's total offense record, Taylor had his choice of scholarship offers from top football programs across the country. But there was something different about the man from Nebraska that struck Taylor.

"A lot of coaches promise you a lot of things as far as starting, playing, and even gifts," says Taylor. "The day he came to my high school, I'll never forget. We were standing outside the gymnasium. When I first met Coach Osborne, he said, 'Steve, I want you to play quarterback, and I'm going to give you the chance to get a good education.' That's what he offered me. The majority of other coaches promised me the world — playing time, starting, and all of this stuff. When he said that, I knew he had my best interest at heart. He said, 'You're going to get what you work for. We're going to give you the opportunity to be the best football player and the best student you can be.'

"That was it. That's all it took. Of course, Nebraska was Nebraska as far as the record on the field, but that was the difference between him and all the other coaches that recruited me.

"I appreciated his sincerity. He was just so genuine. I said, 'Coach, I'm going to Nebraska.' I basically committed right there."

Taylor says he remains thankful for his coach helping make the decision easy to attend Nebraska, a place where Osborne helped him "learn how to be a leader." During his career, Taylor earned All-American honors and is widely considered one of the top quarterbacks ever to play at Nebraska, along with Turner Gill and Tommie Frazier.

The honesty and sincerity that impressed Taylor the first time he met Osborne at his high school have built a strong bond that remains to this day.

"The thing about Coach Osborne is that he treated every player the same when it came to honesty, integrity, and his expectations," Taylor says. "Then again, he also knew the different personalities of players, how to approach them, and what was best for the team. He came across as a guy you could almost talk to as a friend, and then he was always there for you as a coach. To some players, he was there as a father figure, so he just epitomizes what a coach is all about.

"It was always a very comfortable environment. You felt like you could talk to Coach Osborne regardless of the situation. Whether you had a great game or a poor game, he treated you the same.

(continued on next page)

"That builds a total amount of trust and confidence in the coach. It makes you want to give your all for him. It creates a great team atmosphere and chemistry. I think that was the best thing. He treated you the same from the first day he met you until you signed your multimillion-dollar contract, whether you graduated or you didn't graduate. That's why all of us always feel welcome when we come back to Nebraska."

Osborne communicated with care. His team members knew he had their best interest at heart and would always put the team first. He did something else that was special: he gave his team a voice. He empowered his team members — a reliable method for earning buy-in to a program. Osborne was able to give his team members a voice in two different ways: first, through individual conversations, and second, by establishing a group of representatives from the team called the unity council. This council gathered feedback from their teammates and met regularly with Osborne to share it. This system enabled the coaches to keep a finger on the team's pulse, and knowing their concerns gave the coaching staff the opportunity to address them accordingly.

Osborne describes his method: "First of all, I would meet formally with every player in the spring, usually after spring ball. I didn't just talk about football. I talked about their academics, I talked about anything that might be going on with their family, and I certainly talked about what I was seeing on the football field. Maybe more important, every day after practice, players would go into the weight room, and they would maybe have 20 minutes of lifting that they would do. I would usually go in there most days and do a little lifting myself — not much, but some. The process of being there with them on their turf — they weren't being called into my office — meant that I was able to have an average of three, four, or five conversations every night with various players. These informal conversations were about the math class they were having trouble with or if their dad was sick or if their high school team won a big game. I think in the process of a season we would probably have some interaction with most every player at least three, four, five, or six times. It was a conversation that wasn't directly related to their performance on the football field, so I think that was an important time.

"We also established a unity council. The players elected representatives from each position on the team. That sort of gave the players a voice, and these members of the council would bring things up to me that I probably would never otherwise hear about. They were upset about what they had for lunch. Nobody would ever come into your office and say they didn't like what they served for lunch, but you would get feedback. Then, I could get up in front of them after hearing what issues the unity council brought up. It would usually be five or six separate things. They met every week, so I would get up in a team meeting and say, 'We won't have that for lunch again. We'll let you select the movie before we play Missouri. I won't pick it. You can pick it.' Most things could be addressed quickly. There might be something where they'd want to wear Adidas shoes instead of Nike or vice versa. I'd say, 'We have a contract, and we really can't do that.' I think sometimes you were able to put out a lot of minor brush fires that way and have the pulse or the mood of your team translated to you a little bit better. It was at least a way of communication that I thought was helpful."

DICK GOULD: Delivering the Right Message

Tim Mayotte was a player who needed to be nudged. This winner of the 1981 NCAA singles title knew that his coach at Stanford, Dick Gould, expected him at the court for practice whether it was raining or not. "I would take a nap before practice," he recalls. "So many times I would wake up, call, and say, 'Dick, it's raining.' He would always say, 'Tim, it never rains on practice day. Come on down.' I'd say, 'Damn it, Dick, it's raining!' How do you deal with that? You'd go down there, and sure enough, you'd get a practice in."[1]

Other times Gould (in photo above with John McEnroe), retired head coach of the Stanford men's tennis team, used a different means of communication: pure trickery. Mayotte recalls a Gould tactic that surprised teammate Scott Bondurant. "It was a really big match versus UCLA," Mayotte says. "Third set, Bon Man is serving to Bruce Brescia at 5–4. The score is 3-all. We played no-ad, so this is match point for the team. Gouldie got into that position where he's bent over with his hands on his knees. He calls Bon Man over. Scott's waiting for Dick to say some strategy. Finally, he says, 'Dick, what do you want?'

"'Nothing,' Gouldie says. 'I just wanted to intimidate Brescia. Throw the serve into the box. Brescia is going to miss it.' Scott served it five miles per hour and Brescia hit it into the net. We won the match."[2]

Mayotte adds, "The other thing I don't like is players playing not to lose. I think that's really, really important. It doesn't mean you don't play with caution or you just play with reckless abandon. Some players are better when they do that, but overall, no. I think you have to instill a joy in competing and not worrying about the results so much. 'Here's the challenge; let's take this thing and see what we can do with it, as a team and as an individual.'"[3]

Mike Bryan, half of the remarkable doubles combination that is now ranked number one in the world, recalls advice he received from Gould before playing in the 2005 U.S. Open. In a telephone message, Gould said, "Go take it, it's all about you guys." Mike got the message loud and clear: "That means don't rely on your opponents to just give it to you."[4] Alex O'Brien felt similarly. He said, "[Gould] did a great job of making you get out of your comfort zone. Especially when the match was moving against you, so we practiced that a lot."

With certain individuals, Gould preferred a hands-off approach. For example, he never had a problem motivating all-time great John McEnroe. The year after leaving Stanford to turn pro, McEnroe remarked, "My greatest strength is that I have no weaknesses." Another athlete that rose to any challenge was Roscoe Tanner, who with Sandy Mayer helped to lead Stanford to the national title in 1973. Tanner would also go on to an outstanding professional career. "Roscoe's greatness was that he saw the glass overflowing — never half full," said Gould. "He just couldn't understand that other athletes might be his equal. It was pure confidence."[5]

Alex O'Brien, who won the singles, doubles, and team national championships in 1992, was a different type of player. "I was always so hard on myself. He would say, 'O'B, you're doing a really great job out there. You are fighting really hard. I like your attitude.' He would never get on me, because I was always hard on myself. Some of the other guys were a little softer. He'd get out there and just start getting on them. It was really funny listening to him. He did it in a way that wasn't mean spirited. He's basically just trying to help everyone. I think everyone understood that, and nobody took it to a point where it was personal."

Gould agrees that he had to come down hard sometimes on certain players "to wake them up and get them out of what they're doing." Nor did he shy away from disciplining players when their temper overcame their steady play, a common occurrence in tennis. Jim Hodges, who graduated in 1980, recalls an incident during practice that typifies Gould's light hand in discipline. "I was not doing well," Hodges says. "I chucked my racquet into the side of the fence." Gould called to him, "Jimmy, Jimmy! Come here. I want you to meet somebody." Still angry, Hodges stalked over. "This is Andy Geiger," Gould said, "our new athletic director." Hodges immediately got the point. "That was all he did," Hodges says. "I felt about an inch tall."[6] Gould faced a unique challenge in effective communication when Mike and Bob Bryan, identical twins, joined the program. Their coach had trouble telling them apart. "I just addressed them both as 'Hey, Champ,'" he recalls. "Other

(continued on next page)

than one of them being a lefty" — that would be Bob — "I never really got to where I thought of them as two separate people."[7]

He also let his reputation do the talking sometimes. "It got to the point where we had some trophies in our trophy room. Players would walk in and see these and feel a responsibility, so you didn't have to say much once we started winning, which was really, really nice. It took the pressure off having to say that was our goal."

That also helped him with his recruiting. Kids wanted to come to Stanford because it was flat-out the best place to be. "It's not a hard place to sell, especially once we got going. You start out saying, 'Come here. Be the first.' That really appealed to Roscoe." After a while, he saw that the school's winning tradition was built on three pillars. "Number one, the players had to enjoy their experience here. They had to get better while they were at Stanford, and they had to do well in the pro world after they left Stanford. If those three things happened — if they enjoyed their experience, did well at Stanford, and did well beyond Stanford — then it was really an easy sell."

Gould was talented at delivering messages in a timely and effective manner, varying his delivery to match the situation. Delivering a message effectively is one aspect of communication. Another key component of effective communication involves being a good listener. In the caring chapter, you read about mindful conversations. It's important to be present in the moment when you are talking with your team members. If you talk with one of them but it appears that you are merely going through the motions and not taking the time to truly listen, you may have done more damage than good.

Chapter 3

KEEP IT SIMPLE

"LIFE IS REALLY SIMPLE, BUT WE INSIST ON MAKING IT COMPLICATED."
— CONFUCIOUS

Keep it simple. What exactly is "it," you ask? Well, "it" is what you stand for. "It" refers to your expectations. Your formula for success. Right about now you're probably thinking, "How on earth am I supposed to keep that simple?" Fair question, but you will find a way. Consider the things you learned in grade school that you still remember. The stuff you learned that stuck was probably easy to remember because your teacher found a way to make it memorable. Images, acronyms, stories . . . Do that with your coaching philosophy. Make it memorable. Make it stick.

Coach Lou Holtz, of Notre Dame football acclaim, was a master at making his expectations easy to remember and his philosophy stick. The University at Buffalo football program achieved a monumental turnaround operating under Coach Turner Gill's BELIEVE philosophy, which was inspired by tenets he learned under National Championship coach Tom Osborne. Legendary UCLA coach John Wooden found a way to simplify his coaching beliefs by creating his renowned Pyramid of Success.

Find a way to make the most important philosophy stick. When you decide what's most critical for your team to remember, do everything you can to help them encode it in a meaningful way. Tell stories about how it makes a difference in competition. Talk about how it builds character and leads to success in life, not just sports. Make a sign or illustration and post it in the locker room, in the hallways, in meeting rooms, on office walls. You may even want to consider having it stamped on their gear. Mention it often at practice and in meetings. Use examples to illustrate how you want members of your team to act on it. And when they do act on it, reinforce it like crazy. Get your team to buy into your philosophy.

Dick Gould, longtime collegiate tennis coach who earned 17 team national championships during his tenure at Stanford, had expectations for his team members on and off the tennis court. They were simply put, but not always easy to uphold. On the court, he programmed his team members to use an attacking form of serve-and-volley play that at the time was the primary method of winning championships. This active style of play corresponded to his expectations off the court as well: no procrastination and no alibis. When you have something to do, get it done. And don't make excuses.

Turner Gill, former head football coach at Buffalo and Kansas and the new head football coach at Liberty University, still speaks to his college football coach, Tom Osborne, regularly on the phone. When Gill was being recruited by coaches from top programs around the country, he felt something different, something special from Osborne.

COACHING WISDOM

"I honestly felt like he thought it was important for me to graduate from college, be a good person, then be a good football player, in that order."

— Lake Dawson, former Notre Dame football player,
about Lou Holtz

"Integrity and genuineness, those were the two things that sold me," Gill says. "He was a guy I knew would make me a better man; I knew he would make me a better person. For example, his wife came with him on one of his home visits. They had a function together, but he still didn't have to bring her to the house. She was [near Gill's Fort Worth, Texas, home] to go to some function, but she came by the house. That made an impression on me and my whole family. But again, the biggest thing was who [Osborne] was. I knew what I was getting. And, without question, during my four years as a player I saw his genuineness and integrity, and he didn't waver. That's even more powerful.

"I think the biggest thing was that Coach Osborne didn't use any foul language. That was probably the one thing that stood out the most, as well as his demeanor, his poise, self-control. He was the same whether things were going great or not so great. You knew what you were getting. He didn't let outside circumstances dictate how he was going to respond or not respond. He was not going to change his response because of a circumstance. He was who he was. It comes back to those same two words — genuineness and integrity."

Gill, a quarterback at Nebraska, finished as a finalist for the Heisman Trophy, which is given to the top player in college football. A few years later, Osborne served as one of the groomsmen in Gill's wedding. The seeds were planted for Gill's BELIEVE (trademark pending) mission statement during his years as a player for — and a coach alongside — Osborne. And while Osborne clearly exhibited characteristics and an approach that Gill valued, Osborne didn't have a motto or slogan that encompassed his core values and philosophy and anchored his program. Gill set out to do just that, completing his BELIEVE mission statement in 2005 while he served as the director of player development and an offensive assistant with the Green Bay Packers. In December of 2005, he was hired as the head football coach at the University at Buffalo (New York), and BELIEVE changed the culture of the football program there when Gill was hired. The Buffalo football program had won a meager total of ten games in its first seven years in NCAA Division 1. In Gill's third season, the team won eight games and brought home a conference championship. BELIEVE stands for these main tenets:

Believe in each other and things not yet seen

Empower people by encouragement

Learn and press on towards the goal

Influence by being a positive role model

Expect great effort all the time

Visualize excellence

Enjoy the college football experience*

The acronym is easy to remember and stands alone as a solid theme. When Gill was announced as the next University of Kansas head football coach in December 2009, one of the Buffalo team's top players, Dane Robinson, wrote this Facebook message, which was read during Gill's introductory press conference: "He has transformed everything we do here at Buffalo, how we carry ourselves, how we view the game of football, and how we view ourselves as football players. If he has taught us anything here at UB, it was to believe — believe in ourselves, believe in this program, and believe in each other."

A member of Gill's first recruiting class, tight end Kyle Brey, had a unique perspective on the power of Gill's mission statement and how it changed the culture of the downtrodden Buffalo football program. Brey grew up surrounded by top collegiate coaches, as his father, Mike Brey, is currently the head men's basketball coach at Notre Dame. Mike played for and served as an assistant coach under legendary high school basketball coach Morgan Wootten at DeMatha High School in Hyattsville, Maryland, where Wootten coached for 46 years, amassing a career record of 1,274-192. Mike also coached eight seasons as an assistant alongside Mike Krzyzewski at Duke, where he helped them make six NCAA Final Four appearances and win two national championships.

So, when Kyle Brey was considering where to accept a scholarship to play football, he listened to his dad.

*The BELIEVE mission statement is reprinted with generous permission of Turner Gill.

Kyle says, "My dad told me, "you will not only be playing football for a good coach (if you go to Buffalo), you'll be playing for a great man who will help make you a better person.' And that's exactly what happened. We just happened to win a championship along the way, when no one outside of Turner Gill believed we could."

Gill's BELIEVE mission statement was posted in the football offices and meeting-room areas and also recited by players, from memory, at the end of each practice.

"As soon as Turner got there, he wanted to make sure the new freshmen that he brought in understood the BELIEVE mission statement more than anyone, because we were the ones who were going to be there the longest," says Brey, who after graduating from Buffalo in 2010, joined Gill's staff at Kansas as the Quality Control Coach for Special Teams. "Even though we didn't win a lot of games our first year (2-10 record), this wasn't going to change in a year. Whether we won the championship or lost the championship, this is going to take multiple years to change the mindset that the whole University at Buffalo had.

"The great thing about Buffalo is we didn't have a lot of talented guys. We had a lot of guys who wanted to work really hard. Believing in what Turner was saying everyday was such a blind faith because there was no evidence to support we were ever going to win. There was nothing to do but believe, because everyone thought we were going to lose anyway. I knew I was going to go there, I was probably going to lose every game my whole career, but at least was I going to get a division one scholarship.

COACHING WISDOM

"Success is peace of mind that is the direct result of self-satisfaction in knowing you did your best to become the best that you are capable of becoming."

— John Wooden's definition of Success

"But we got together, listened to Coach Gill, and said, 'Hey, why don't we just believe?' At Buffalo, we were looking to take a step that had never been taken and we needed someone to say, 'Hey, we can take this step now, you earned it, it's fine. I know what it's like to take this step, and let's do it together.' And we believed in him, we bought into the mission statement, and we took that step."

Follow Turner Gill's example and find a way to make your most important philosophy stick. You may not be able to eliminate playbooks, and you might still have to hand out extensive policies and procedures manuals. But you can distill those down to the main points and communicate the key values of your program in a memorable way. Think back to your first day on the job — did you feel overwhelmed by new information? A barrage of information is tough for most people to sift through. When an individual needs to make an important decision, there isn't always time to refer back to the manual. Members of your team will make decisions based on the messages you have drilled into them over and over — the basics that you have insisted upon. This is true with technique on the playing field, and it's also true when it comes to personal choices off the field, in relationships, in academics, in life. Find a way to let your team members know: This is what we stand for, here's the expectation, here's who I am and what I expect.

Legendary UCLA men's basketball coach John Wooden created and refined the Pyramid of Success over many years to illustrate the key principles he believed led to excellence in sports and in life. Wooden grew up on a farm in Centerton, Indiana. Wooden's father, Joshua, set clear rules for his four boys. Joshua shared his "two sets of threes" with his sons:

Never lie. Never cheat. Never steal.

and

Don't whine. Don't complain. Don't make excuses.

"I've remembered those two sets of threes since the first time dad shared them with me," Wooden said. "And I've worked hard to follow them my entire life."

With those rules as his anchor, the first seeds of his Pyramid of Success were planted when he received an assignment from his math teacher at Martinsville (Indiana) High School. The students were supposed to write a paper defining success. He turned the paper in, but the assignment was far from completed in Wooden's mind.

In 1934, Wooden settled on a definition of success, which serves as the apex of his Pyramid of Success. His definition reads, "Success is peace of mind that is the direct result of self-satisfaction in knowing you did your best to become the best that you are capable of becoming."

"Through the years, my belief in that definition has grown stronger," Wooden said. "Success is about striving to achieve your personal best. And only you know that. Only you know if you gave it your all to become the best that you could become. I may look at you and think, *wow, that person is really working hard*, but only you know if you've given it your all. Winning a game, a national championship, are by-products of success, not success itself."

CHALK TALK:

X **IDENTIFY THE MAIN PRINCIPLES THAT ARE MOST IMPORTANT FOR YOUR TEAM MEMBERS TO REMEMBER.**

O **USE A VARIETY OF METHODS TO DRILL YOUR PHILOSOPHY INTO THEIR MEMORY: VISUAL AIDS, REPETITION, ACRONYMS, STORIES, AND EXAMPLES.**

X **PROVIDE POSITIVE REINFORCEMENT WHEN YOU SEE PLAYERS PUTTING THESE PHILOSOPHIES INTO ACTION.**

O **HIGHLIGHT THE IMPORTANCE OF THESE PRINCIPLES OUTSIDE OF SPORTS.**

PROFILES

JOHN WOODEN: Achieving Excellence

John Wooden didn't move one frame, change one curtain, or repaint the color of the walls after his dear wife, Nell, passed away on March 21, 1985. Nell had decorated their condominium just so, and keeping the place the same helped Wooden (with Kareem Abdul-Jabbar in photo at left) maintain the strong, undying love he had for his wife, to whom he wrote a love letter on the 21st of each month for the rest of his life.

In Wooden's den, framed pictures and proclamations in his honor rested on the carpeted floor against the wall. This humble spot is where he kept the framed display of the Presidential Medal of Freedom Award he was given by President George W. Bush in 2003, the highest honor a United States citizen can receive. Above the television hung the ten NCAA national championship plaques that his UCLA teams won.

"What do you notice about the plaques?" Wooden asked me.

Once you grasp that Wooden led his teams to ten national championships — six more than the next closest college basketball coaches, Adolph Rupp and Mike Krzyzewski — you notice that the plaques hang to make a unique shape.

"They make a pyramid," Wooden said, smiling. "That was Nell's idea, and it pleases me very much."

The design is in honor of the "Pyramid of Success," a visual representation of Wooden's values and the expectations he had for his team, a concept he labored for years to define and construct. The fact that there are enough plaques to construct a pyramid — four on the bottom, three on the next row above it, two more above that, and one on top — is testament to the fact that the principles and characteristics emphasized in his Pyramid of Success helped his teams achieve excellence.

Wooden's desk in his den held a neat stack of copies of the Pyramid of Success, with a few black and a few blue fine-point Sharpies alongside them. Wooden personally signed thousands of copies of the Pyramid of Success throughout the years for anyone who wrote him a letter requesting one. He was honored that people across the country maintained interest in his creation, decades after he first considered the definition of success in his high school math class.

DICK GOULD: Teaching an Aggressive Technique

Dick Gould (with Jared Palmer in photo above) taught a style of tennis technique to several generations of players. "I made my living by an attacking game. Physically, most (junior) players are just not strong enough to serve and volley, to get in off the return at the net. Maybe they can volley, maybe they can't, but most of them, including McEnroe and Alex, were basically baseliners. By the time they come to college at 17 or 18 years old, they're bigger and stronger. My job was to transform them as much as possible into an attacking serve-and-volley player, someone who would make something happen, rather than react to something that was happening."

Alex O'Brien knows how much that style helped him. "I remember when I first came to Stanford, I sure wasn't very good. The only time I came to the net was really to shake hands. He taught me how to serve and how to volley," he says. Gould "forced me to do it and forced me to play aggressively. As I grew and matured, it added a whole new element to my game. Typically, I would saddle the match from the baseline and not have very many options. He helped me create more discomfort for my opponent by attacking them at a time when they wouldn't expect it."

Gould favored an attacking style for another reason as well. The standard playing surface in college was the hard court, so common today but not as standard back then. Under Gould's tutelage, John McEnroe took advantage of that shift. "My serve-and-volley game developed even further when I went to Stanford because, for the first time in my life, I was playing nothing but hard-court tennis. Suddenly, I saw the serve and volley was the better way to play."[1]

As times changed, though, Gould did, too. "Now the game's changed a little bit. The first player I had who didn't win the NCAA by serving and volleying was Bobby Bryan in 1998. He was basically not a serve-and-volleyer, but until that time everybody who won the NCAA championship won by [that technique]," he said. He saw the game evolving into the style seen so often today. "There started to be more topspin and back-courters. It became harder to teach [serve and volley] because the pros were having success without doing it."

Gould does have some hard rules about a player's approach to the game. "I can't stand procrastination. I can't stand alibis. These are constants. I hate when people don't accept responsibility for something they've done or they don't take charge of something they have to do and do it."

LOU HOLTZ

LOU HOLTZ: The WIN Philosophy

Lou Holtz smiles as he leans forward in the bright blue leather chair in the family room of his elegant and spacious Orlando home. "I'm not very smart," he says, "so I've always tried to simplify life to the best of my ability."

Holtz commands high dollars on the corporate speaking circuit and entertains millions of viewers weekly with his wit and humor on ESPN throughout the college football season. He clearly doesn't give himself enough credit for his intellectual prowess. Nonetheless, keeping it simple has served him well.

Holtz led six college football programs as a head coach, and he had the same three rules for every one of them:

Do right.

Do everything to the best of your ability.

Make sure people know you care about them.

Overly simple? Coach Holtz won a national championship with those rules.

Do right. Do everything to the best of your ability. Make sure people know you care about them. When you think about it, Coach Holtz's three simple rules cover just about any sort of misbehavior you could imagine might need to be addressed. "Do right" is an easy thing for team members to remember when they are faced with tough decisions. It emphasizes the importance of having a moral compass. Nearly all of us have had someone in our lives — a parent, a teacher, a coach, a grandparent, a sibling, a mentor, a friend — who helped develop and amplify the voice of our conscience. Lou Holtz's "Do right" rule provided a guidepost for his players, so they'd listen to that voice. And he made it clear that this rule was necessary if a person wanted to be successful and have meaningful relationships in life.

"If you do the right thing, you are always going to have trust," Holtz says. "All relationships start with trust. You can't have a relationship with a wife, a child, or an athlete if it's not based on trust. They don't have to like you, but they have to be able to trust you. If you do the right thing, you're going to have trust."

Coach Holtz's second rule, "Do everything to the best of your ability," is also going to build trust among teammates and coaches. And Holtz insists that people should aim to do their best even when no one is watching and there is no reward. He posed a challenge to his players, "Are you committed to excellence? You can talk about being great, but have you done everything you can to make that program the best you can?"

Coach Holtz's third rule is about caring, a key ingredient to coaching greatness that was described in detail in the first chapter of this book. Holtz says, "The last thing is you have to let people know you genuinely care." In addition to expecting this of his players, he views this as a critical skill for coaches. And he clarifies exactly what he means by caring for players:

"Caring is not being their friend. They don't need a friend. Caring about them is preparing them for the difficult things that they are going to encounter in the game and in life. That was the basis of what we did."

Three simple rules.

Three rules, and the WIN philosophy.

Do you have a coaching philosophy? A life philosophy? If not, consider adopting Lou Holtz's WIN philosophy. WIN stands for "What's Important Now?" The WIN philosophy focuses on the everyday details that lead to bigger achievements.

"So many people say they wish this would happen, they wish that would happen," Holtz says. "I think when you focus on what you want in your life, you ask yourself 25 times a day, 'What's important now?' You wake up in the morning. What's important now? Get out of bed. You want to be a good student. What's important now? You go to class, sit in the front, get your notebook and pen out, and pay attention. So you see that when you focus on what's important now, you evaluate the past, focus on the future, and it tells you what to do in the present."

What's important now? Lake Dawson still asks himself that question, nearly 20 years after he played wide receiver for Coach Lou Holtz at the University of Notre Dame. Coach Holtz wanted his team members to focus on taking care of the details of the moment — knowing the play, getting the assignments correct, giving 100 percent. Worrying about the past or thinking too far ahead could distract them from what they needed to do in the present. So he told them to remember the acronym "WIN." And it stuck with Lake for life.

Holtz, now 74, still gets calls or letters from four or five of his former players every week. Most, he says, can still do an impression of him, lisp and all. He also hears how the WIN philosophy and the three rules have made an impact in their lives.

He wants them to know it made an impact in his life as well.

"The other side of the three rules we had for our teams is the questions that every one of our players asked us as coaches: 'Can I trust you? Are you committed? Do you care about me?'" Holtz says. "That was our commitment to them.

"On every [bowl] ring we had at Notre Dame, you'll find 'Trust, Love,

(continued on next page)

Commitment.' Those were our core values, and I made sure we stayed true to them."

Today, inside Gate D of Notre Dame Stadium, which has been designated national championship coaches gate, stands a statue of Holtz flanked by two players. The pedestal reads:

Lou Holtz
Head Coach
1986–1996
100 WINS, 30 LOSSES, 2 TIES
NATIONAL CHAMPIONSHIP 1988
"TRUST, LOVE, COMMITMENT"

Lake Dawson not only invested himself fully into Holtz's rules and overall philosophy on achieving your personal best as a student-athlete while at Notre Dame, he still lives by them today.

Dawson was a part of Holtz's recruiting class at Notre Dame in 1990. That group of freshmen, to this day, is considered one of the top classes of football student-athletes in Notre Dame history. After winning 40 games during their four years, five men from that class were picked in the first round of the 1994 NFL draft.

"There were two big reason I bought into Coach Holtz from the beginning," says Dawson, a big-play wide receiver at Notre Dame who, after five years of playing in the NFL, is now the Vice President of Football Operations with the Tennessee Titans. "I did well as a player from our first training camp during freshman year, and also because he made me feel like he cared about me," said Dawson. "I honestly felt like he thought it was important for me to graduate from college, be a good person, then be a good football player, in that order.

"And along with the three rules he talked about, something that stands out to me to this day is Coach Holtz's WIN philosophy — What's important now?" The impact of the WIN philosophy still lives within Dawson today.

"He'd say it's the same philosophy applied to life and school," Dawson says. "In your profession, it's not just about the workload itself, because he was saying when you look at the big picture of it, you would get discouraged. Taking it action by action was one of his ideas that he stressed. It's something that I've used myself after college, applied it as a professional athlete and now in my role in the NFL, taking care of the little things every day that will lead to taking care of the big things. I even talk to my kids about the WIN philosophy."

JOHN WOODEN: Building the Pyramid of Success

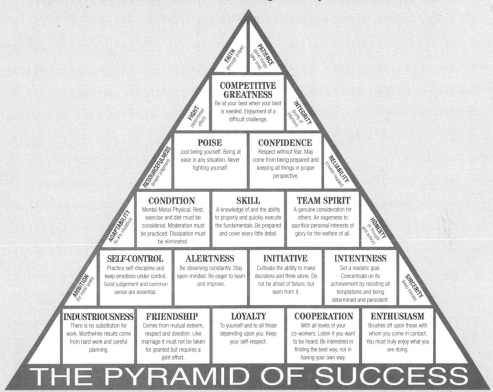

The Pyramid of Success

- **FAITH** (through prayer)
- **PATIENCE** (good things take time)
- **FIGHT** (determined effort)
- **INTEGRITY** (purity of intention)
- **RESOURCEFULNESS** (proper judgment)
- **RELIABILITY** (creates respect)
- **ADAPTABILITY** (to any situation)
- **HONESTY** (in thought and action)
- **AMBITION** (for noble goals)
- **SINCERITY** (keep friends)

COMPETITIVE GREATNESS — Be at your best when your best is needed. Enjoyment of a difficult challenge.

POISE — Just being yourself. Being at ease in any situation. Never fighting yourself.

CONFIDENCE — Respect without fear. May come from being prepared and keeping all things in proper perspective.

CONDITION — Mental-Moral-Physical. Rest, exercise and diet must be considered. Moderation must be practiced. Dissipation must be eliminated.

SKILL — A knowledge of and the ability to properly and quickly execute the fundamentals. Be prepared and cover every little detail.

TEAM SPIRIT — A genuine consideration for others. An eagerness to sacrifice personal interests of glory for the welfare of all.

SELF-CONTROL — Practice self-discipline and keep emotions under control. Good judgement and common sense are essential.

ALERTNESS — Be observing constantly. Stay open-minded. Be eager to learn and improve.

INITIATIVE — Cultivate the ability to make decisions and think alone. Do not be afraid of failure, but learn from it.

INTENTNESS — Set a realistic goal. Concentrate on its achievement by resisting all temptations and being determined and persistent.

INDUSTRIOUSNESS — There is no substitution for work. Worthwhile results come from hard work and careful planning.

FRIENDSHIP — Comes from mutual esteem, respect and devotion. Like marriage it must not be taken for granted but requires a joint effort.

LOYALTY — To yourself and to all those depending upon you. Keep your self-respect.

COOPERATION — With all levels of your co-workers. Listen if you want to be heard. Be interested in finding the best way, not in having your own way.

ENTHUSIASM — Brushes off upon those with whom you come in contact. You must truly enjoy what you are doing.

THE PYRAMID OF SUCCESS

Denny Crum holds the unique distinction to have played for John Wooden at UCLA, served as an assistant coach with Wooden at UCLA, and coached against Wooden. Crum's Louisville team lost to UCLA in Wooden's next-to-last game as head coach at UCLA, two days before UCLA won their final national championship under Wooden's leadership.

Crum, who won two national championships as the head coach at Louisville (one of only 13 coaches in college basketball history to win multiple championships), remembers the Pyramid of Success as a player at UCLA in the late 1950s.

"He never pushed the Pyramid on us as players, but the characteristics and blocks of the Pyramid were stressed every day," Crum says. "Coach had a large Pyramid of Success on the wall of his office, he had one on his desk, so it was always there as a backdrop to our program. But more than that, he stressed the principles contained in the Pyramid. I knew as a player, and later as a coach, that I was expected to bring my best every day to contribute to help our team become the best it could be."

(continued on next page)

Crum displayed the Pyramid of Success in his office during his 30-year career as head coach at Louisville, and thereafter in his fundraising role with the university.

Following his father's tradition of threes, Wooden required that his team members follow three simple rules that were closely tied to blocks of his Pyramid:

Never be late. ["Industriousness"]

Not one word of profanity. ["Self-Control"]

Never criticize a teammate. ["Team Spirit"]

And it's of interest to note that in the 15 years Wooden spent perfecting the Pyramid, the two cornerstones never changed. They are Industriousness and Enthusiasm.

"Whether it be a building, or a person's mental state, the foundation that it rests on is most important," Wooden said. "The cornerstones always stayed the same because there is no substitute for hard work. And to work hard at something, you have to embrace it and enjoy it, which brings out your best effort. I stressed this with all my players on every team I coached."

Entire books have been dedicated to exploring the Pyramid of Success. Below is an in-depth look at the Pyramid of Success, with thoughts that John Wooden shared with me during our first one-on-one interview more than six years before he died on June 4, 2010.

Industriousness

"You have to work hard to achieve any worthy goal. And do not mistake activity for achievement. One of my favorite poems about this is written by Grantland Rice." John Wooden then proceeded to recite the poem from memory.

How to Be a Champion

You wonder how they do it,
You look to see the knack,
You watch the foot in action,
Or the shoulder or the back.
But when you spot the answer
Where the higher glamours lurk,
You'll find in moving higher
Up the laurel-covered spire,
That most of it is practice,
And the rest of it is work.

Friendship

"With this block of the foundation, I relate it to respect and camaraderie. It doesn't mean that I'm buddy-buddy with those on my team, but it does mean that we're in it together as members of the same team. This mutual respect and care for each other bonds us together and will help make our team stronger."

Loyalty

"A leader needs to be loyal to their organization. They also need to have high standards and values themselves and strive to adhere to them. This will set a good example for those on their team following them."

Cooperation

"So much more can be done when we work together. This is about creating an environment in which people can share their ideas and work together to bring about positive change. I will also say that while we have everyone working together and all will receive praise, it's the leader's role to take the blame and be accountable for any shortcomings. That's very important."

Enthusiasm

"Be excited and care about what you are doing. This shows through to those around you. If you are fully invested, and you do it with all your heart, your team will respond with the same spirit. If they don't, maybe they need to find another place to be. People who love making a contribution to the team like being around others who love making a contribution to the team. Look for those types of people."

Self-Control

"This one was sometimes very challenging. The emotion of a game sometimes got the better of me. I always tried, however, to maintain a sense of control of emotions. When you do this effectively, you can be more focused, more clear minded, so you can do a better job with the situation at hand."

Alertness

"Be aware of your surroundings and you'll learn a lot. Don't be so focused on what is right in front of you and miss what is happening around you. You can learn a lot by working on this skill."

(continued on next page)

JOHN WOODEN

Initiative

"Don't be afraid to try something new, or take a different approach to an old situation or problem. I think of making mistakes of commission and mistakes of omission. Usually, teams that achieve more make more mistakes of commission, because they are trying their best to make something happen, not just sit back and wait for something to happen."

Intentness

"Focus on what's important and keep moving toward that goal. Maintain your competitiveness and determination on striving every day to meet your goal."

Condition

"By this, I mean moral, mental, and physical condition. It's all related. I believe the most important word in the dictionary is 'love.' Second is 'balance.' Balance is important in everything you do. This affects the decisions we make. I used to tell my teams:

There is a choice you have to make,
In everything you do.
So keep in mind, that in the end,
The choice you make, makes you."

Skill

"You have to have the skill, to have a mastery of what you're doing, and be able to do it efficiently to achieve consistently. It takes great effort to master a skill. It doesn't come easy."

Team Spirit

"Simply putting the team first. That is the definition of a team player. I always preferred having a team player who made the team great than just having a great player."

Poise

"Being secure in who you are regardless of the situation. It could be good or bad, but poise helps you maintain a sense of balance. There's balance again, an ability to withstand whatever is happening externally and maintain your conviction."

Confidence

"Having a strong belief in yourself and your abilities. But you need to be careful, because there is a difference between confidence and arrogance. My dad told us, "You're just as good as anyone, but no better than anyone.""

Competitive Greatness

"This can only be achieved through the constant, day-to-day effort to become the best you are capable of becoming. It's not easy to achieve Competitive Greatness. It's really challenging, in fact. There is no simple formula to achieve it. "

"The principles of the Pyramid are simple," Wooden said. "Following them might not always be easy, but the principles that will lead you to success are simple."

Chapter 4

BUILDING TEAM-FIRST UNITY

"A SUCCESSFUL TEAM BEATS WITH ONE HEART."
— UNKNOWN

How do you get all the individuals on your team to buy into the team mission? In sports, in business, and in life, this can be a big challenge. Especially when your team consists of talented individuals who have already experienced plenty of success on their own. A team full of stars may have extraordinary capabilities, but if individuals are out for themselves, the team will not perform to its full potential. If you are familiar with the story of the U.S.A. Olympic hockey team's gold-medal season in 1980, you understand the value of building a team of role-players. Coach Herb Brooks knew exactly what he was doing when he pieced together his gold-medal team. People doubted his method at first, wondering why he would pass over certain talented players in favor of others who were selected. But Coach Brooks knew something they didn't. He knew the winning potential of a group of individuals that would put the team first.

So how do you accomplish that? Personnel selection is step one. Gather as much information as you can about individuals before inviting them to join your team. Ask as many people as you can about their character. What motivates this person? How does he or she react to disappointment? What kind of team member does this person choose to be? Has this person ever taken on a different role to benefit the team? If so, how did he or she handle that situation? Past behavior is the best predictor of future behavior. You want to assemble a team that is comprised of people who are willing to contribute in whatever way will best serve the team goal, even if their role is not as glamorous as they'd hoped or as significant as they'd expected.

No college program has captivated sports fans more in recent history than the underdog Butler Bulldogs men's basketball team. Butler, led by head coach Brad Stevens, epitomizes the team-first philosophy.

Stevens used his experiences as a player — which you'll read more about shortly —to shape his recruiting efforts at Butler. He and his staff specifically target individuals who will buy into the team-first philosophy. Former NFL coach Tony Dungy, who steered the Indianapolis Colts to a Super Bowl victory in 2007, was also very selective about which prospects were invited to join the Indianapolis Colts team.

Coach Dungy explains, "We focused on character, and we were very fortunate in an NFL process where you get to do that. You go through and evaluate in a lot of different areas, and that was one that we tried to evaluate. We tried to get our scouts to do a lot of research. We talked to not only the coaches, but to academic advisers, high school teachers, people in their community where they grew up, and a lot of people around the university that weren't athletes. We did those background checks. We had an interview process that was important to us. Guys who we were really strongly considering, we would bring in and talk to them and try to get our assistant coaches to get a feel for them, if they were going to be the kind of teammates that we were looking for. The letter grade that they got in character was just as important as the letter grade in quickness, speed, agility, strength, all those other factors. It was something that we weighed very heavily. You ask them what's important in their life, what their goals are, what they see themselves doing, and you're always looking for guys who are not just saying, 'Oh, I want to be a Pro Bowl player. I want to be the best that I can be.' Obviously, you want that. That has to be part of it, but you're looking for those players who talk about other areas of their life, what they want to do and how they want to be involved in the community.

"The other thing we looked at was academic performance, because a lot of times that can tell you a lot. Everyone likes to play, likes to practice, and likes to lift weights. You ask the strength coach, 'Is this guy a hard worker?' 'Oh, yes he is. He's the greatest worker we've had.' But you may get a totally different answer when you ask the biology professor. Can a guy put in effort at things that he doesn't necessarily like? How important was school to him? You get a sense of that when you look at the transcripts, so academic performance was a factor as well. At one point just before I left, I know we had the second-highest rate of college graduates on our team, behind the Patriots. To me, there's no surprise why those two teams were very good and over a five- or six-year period won a bunch of Super Bowls. There's a correlation when you get guys that are not only high achievers on the field, but in the classroom as well."

Dungy makes an excellent point. Are the individuals you're adding to your team going to work hard no matter what the task entails? How is a person going to react if asked to contribute to the team by doing something he or she doesn't really want to do? People who give back to the community and have goals outside of sports may be more likely to possess a sense of gratitude for their talents, maintain a healthy perspective when adversity hits, and work hard to make the most of their opportunities. Aren't these the people you want on your team?

Yes, says former Notre Dame football coach Lou Holtz. When he was recruiting, he looked for several qualities. "There were basically seven things I wanted. Number one was character and integrity. Two was talent, the ability to succeed academically and athletically. Three, a guy who loved the game and wanted to play football. You didn't have to give him a pep talk to get him to want to go out and practice. Number four, he wanted to do something with his life. There were things he wanted to accomplish in life. Five was the ability to run and move. Six was a guy who was physically tough and mentally tough. The other thing, I wanted a guy who was productive. This guy is 6-foot-2 and he runs a 40 in 4.1 [seconds], but how many passes did he catch? He caught two. Lake Dawson is 6 feet, 180 pounds. He's a 4.6 in the 40, but he caught 78 balls. Who's productive?"

The ability to make things happen.

The world is competitive — in sports, in business, and in life. You want people on your team who possess a strong drive to win.

Granted, that same competitive drive that provides added motivation can also lead people to focus on selfish endeavors, causing them to turn their attention away from what's best for the team. Some individuals are naturals at gracefully owning whatever role they are asked to fill. They give their all at all times, even if that means setting aside their pride and taking on a less exciting task or cheering from the bench. Most individuals will not be graceful about this at first. They may even go through stages of grief if their role shifts to something less glamorous. It is important that you try to understand this adjustment phase. It's reasonable for players to experience difficulty changing up their contribution — whether they are still trying to prove their worth as a newcomer, moving from one position to another, falling on the depth chart, or being asked to groom someone who could take over their position.

Acknowledge and normalize their emotions, and then clearly explain why that decision is best for the team. And if you notice that someone is dwelling on negative emotions to the extent that it is interfering with the team's mission, let the individual know that while you understand the adjustment is tough, it's time to get with the program for the benefit of the team. Give them some time to adjust, but don't allow them to dwell in their own negative emotion.

Legendary UCLA basketball coach John Wooden was a genius at discerning what needed to happen for his team to succeed. And succeed his teams did, over and over again, winning one national championship after another. During his first few seasons coaching at UCLA, however, it was challenging for his team members to adjust to his team-first approach. One player in particular, center George Stanich, recalled having an especially difficult time adapting to the new role Coach Wooden assigned him. But eventually, he embraced his role as a guard on Wooden's team — a role that he certainly would not have chosen for himself but which, he finally recognized, made the team stronger. Wooden cultivated a team-first mentality amongst the individuals who played for him.

"It is amazing how much people get done if they don't worry about who gets the credit."
— Swahili proverb

Brad Stevens has been able to generate that same kind of selflessness on his Butler Bulldogs team, thanks in part to his own firsthand experience on his college basketball team, when he had to accept a less celebrated role than he had originally hoped for. Stevens acknowledges that this helped shape his coaching approach.

"Becoming a good teammate was learned. It was not something that came easily, and I think it's really helped me in coaching. I started some my freshman year but played quite a bit. I started a lot my sophomore year. To be quite honest, what happened was the coach recruited better players. Sometimes that's hard to swallow. When you're in the moment, you don't think that. My junior year was probably pretty difficult in grasping that. At the end of my junior year, I thought to myself, 'Hey, if you're going to do this, you need to do it for the right reasons.'

"I maybe played 20 minutes a game my junior year, maybe 15 my senior year — much, much less than prior years — but I can't tell you how many times I've reflected on it. It is so important to what I'm doing now because I spend a lot more time with guys 8–14 than I do with one through seven (players who receive the most playing time in games), as far as talking about how life is, if they have their internship set up, things that really matter, so they know they're just as important as the person getting all of the headlines.

"It's also good because I understand when a kid goes in the game and he's playing ten minutes a game; I understand that he's trying to be productive. By trying to be productive, he's actually hurting himself and us more, rather than just doing his job. I think it's a positive thing that I'm able to say that I've sat there and I understand why he's doing it. It's something that every kid has to go through. You have to *learn* to be a great teammate. You have to be willing to be a great teammate, and I think it's easier at the Division III level because none of us is going to play pro."

Stevens's college coach, Bill Fenlon, agrees that Stevens's experience as a role-player who put the team first at DePauw is an asset that helps him succeed as a coach. "I think people that end up coaching — you see some successful players become pretty good coaches — but there are an awful lot of guys who had to figure out what their role was and really had to understand the chemical aspects of fitting in with the team. It's not a surprise to me that Brad is a successful coach, because he gets what being on a team is about. It's really easy to be the best guy. I always tell our guys that the easy thing is to be the guy who plays all the time. It's really hard to be a guy who doesn't play all the time or doesn't know how much he's going to play or is a little uncertain about his role at times and has to find a way to stay prepared and ready. I think that guy has a chance to learn things about himself that is not so urgent for other guys. When you're that guy, you have to figure out a way to either sacrifice yourself for the good of the program or get lost, because otherwise you're going to be a bad teammate.

"We always talk about accepting your role or you're going to be a bad teammate. You don't necessarily have to be satisfied with your role, which means you are going to come out and compete every day to try to expand your role or change it. When it's time to go out and lock arms with the other guy, you'd better be on board. Brad always figured out a way to do that, and I always really valued that very highly about him. I think sometimes, through athletics and through competition, you have these opportunities. It kind of seems like life and death when you're going through it, but in reality no one is going to die. It's really not the end of the world one way or the other, but because you are in this laboratory you get to find out [things] about yourself. You find out a little bit about what you're made of, and sometimes you might not necessarily like the things you find out. The great thing about it is you can come back the next day and get to change. [Brad's] a guy who really exemplified all of the things about a team we talk about. I know that wasn't always easy for him as a player, because he was a young guy and he's a human being, but I remember everybody's got their goals. Everybody wants what they want. We wouldn't be human if we didn't. That's one of the things that teams teachs us: that you can't always have it the way [you want], so you'd better find another way to make it work for yourself. He was able to do that, and I always appreciated that about him."

How can you help your team members become better team players? A team-first attitude requires cultivation. It is your responsibility to develop a team-first mentality in each of your team members. For some, it will come naturally. With others, you have your work cut out for you. If you lose and you do not have a cohesive group that puts the team first, team members will start finger-pointing and complaining — if not to you then to each other. "Why is so-and-so still getting an opportunity? I can't believe that! Why aren't I getting a chance to show what I can do?" Negative energy will spread through a team faster than wildfire. It is toxic. And toxic teams are not championship teams.

What can you do about it? Well, this might be an unpopular suggestion, but if your players are putting you in the hot seat about your decisions, it doesn't hurt to take another good look at how you're running the team. Remember, the definition of insanity is doing the same thing over and over again and expecting different results. And through that examination process, if you identify anything that you need to do differently, acknowledge that to your team. Explain how the change will help the team. If you sense discontent from the group but feel strongly about keeping things the way they are, you may want to tell them *why* you're sticking with the existing game plan. Right now, you might be thinking, *I shouldn't have to explain myself — I'm in charge.* Hold up, though. Just for a moment, think about parenting styles. As a child, did you ever hear, "Do it because I said so!"? How unsatisfying and infuriating was that command? Explain things so that your team will understand your reasoning. They may not agree with it, but at least they will have an explanation. And each time you choose to explain why you are running a certain play or giving an opportunity to a certain person, you can reiterate that you are making decisions for the good of the team.

Former Stanford tennis coach Dick Gould accomplished the very challenging task of persuading several extremely talented, individually minded athletes to align their own personal goals with the good of the overall team. By preaching a team-first mentality and even giving his team a voice regarding determination of the lineup, he was able to corral them in the right direction. They supported each other and negotiated ways to accept their roles, regardless of whether they were in the number-one spot or the number-four spot in the lineup. This was a formula for success.

Take a moment to consider all the different roles on your team. Are there certain ones that seem more valuable than others? What would happen if one of the "less important" roles was removed from your team? What would your team be missing? Would it change the way things are run?

Truly unified teams are made up of a plethora of individual roles, all of which are integral to the team's success. Not everyone can be the star. But all the members of your team can shine in their own unique way. On nearly every team there is an unequal distribution of glory, and because of that there will be times when certain team members doubt their value. If you are perceived as favoring the top producers, you run the big risk of losing the buy-in of your role-players. And they are just as important to the team's success. It takes everyone. Your job as the one in charge, whether in sports, business, or other arenas in life, is to find ways to honor and value *every* team member's contribution, no matter how small or how unglorified. Make sure all your team members know they are valued.

There are many ways to do this. When you distribute roles, highlight the importance of the ones that are not as coveted. Provide positive reinforcement when players successfully execute their roles, even — and especially — when that means thanking them for being supportive of the team and for being willing to do the little things that often go unrecognized. Create opportunities to publicly recognize the less glorified role-players on your team, perhaps by giving a shout-out to the most valuable supporting role. Having team members vote on this can add even more weight. Because you're in charge, it is your job to demonstrate to the team that each person's role has worth. The team will take its cues from you. If you highlight the value of each role, the rest of the team will value that, too.

When asked what makes the Butler men's basketball program so special, NBA draftee Shelvin Mack talks about the importance of each person understanding and accepting their role in order to help the team. "When we walked out on the court we weren't always the biggest team, we weren't always the fastest team, we weren't always the biggest individuals, but we knew that together as a team we could do great things. In basketball, you always need your teammates to help you. That's Coach Stevens's biggest thing — it's never going to be one guy who is going to go out there and stop one person from scoring. It's a chain reaction. If someone gets beat, someone has to come over and help them out.

"What made us so successful is that everyone knew their role. Most of the guys on our team understood that they weren't going to go on and play professional basketball, but they were okay with that. They knew that their career was going to be in the workforce. So, you had guys who bought in and just contributed and did things the right way. At other schools, you have guys who are worried about going to the NBA, worried about this, worried about that, and don't always think about what's best for the team."

COACHING WISDOM

"[E]verybody had a role to play. The better each person played that role, the better we were going to be as a team."

— Tom Osborne

Nebraska athletic director Tom Osborne, a National Championship–winning coach, made an ongoing effort to highlight the significance of every role on the path to victory. "A lot of these kids that we recruited were the best player on their team, maybe the best player to ever play on their team in the history of their school. All of a sudden they're thrown in with a bunch of other good players. Some of them have to be on the scout team, and some of them don't play a whole lot for a couple of years. You see a lot more moving around; players will come and things aren't quick and easy, so they'll transfer to another school. I guess the thing that we tried to emphasize was that everybody had a role to play. The better each person played that role, the better we were going to be as a team. When the team won, everybody won. If we had an excellent team and we were nationally ranked, going to play for the national championship or in a significant bowl game, then in a sense everybody participated. Everybody benefitted. Everybody won."

A related topic involves treatment of your star players. This is another critical piece of a team-first approach. If you're the one in charge, you need to ask yourself a very important question: Are you willing to sit a star player who does not put the team first? This is one of the strongest ways to send the team-first message to your entire group. Especially if you choose to sit your star player because that person is not on board with the team-first mission. This is a tough decision to make, particularly if your paycheck depends on your team's performance.

College Football Hall of Fame coach Lou Holtz made an unpopular decision when he was the head coach of the Arkansas Razorbacks. Heading into the 1978 Orange Bowl, he suspended his top two running backs and top wide receiver for violating team rules. The team was facing number-two nationally ranked Oklahoma. Holtz took much heat from the Arkansas faithful at the time, but he stood his ground and remained strong in his decision. Holtz's Arkansas Razorbacks won the game 31–6.

Most of the time, people respect a leader who is willing to take action when the team's success is at stake. And if you enact swift and consistent consequences, others typically learn from the example and fall in line. Hopefully, this will not be a frequent occasion. You might see it more often when you are in the midst of implementing a culture shift, particularly when you are taking over an existing program from previous management. Usually, those who do not want to get on board will self-select out or be ousted, and the rest will embrace what you are trying to do. When Don Shula took over as head coach of the Miami Dolphins in 1970, the struggling team welcomed the change. Shula emphasized the team-first philosophy from the beginning, and every detail was hammered home day in and day out, with the ultimate goal of making the Dolphins into the very best team possible.

Shula coached with a desire to continue striving, a belief that one should never become complacent. This is the attitude of sustained success. Of course, even the most successful teams will experience setbacks. And when you truly create a team-first environment, you will find that just as your team members celebrate joyful victories together, they will also support each other through painful losses. This was especially true for the Butler men's basketball program in 2011.

"TEAMS SHARE THE BURDEN AND DIVIDE THE GRIEF."
— DOUG SMITH

The Butler Bulldogs had such a strong bond as a team that they weathered adversity together in a way that many teams might not be able to do. They lifted each other up even at a time when they were feeling incredibly low. Their team-first atmosphere encircled them all, providing comfort and helping them accept a national championship loss with a spirit of gratitude for their team. This level of team cohesion is created over time, starting from day one. There are many different ways to help your team bond as a group. Get past the surface and encourage trust building and sharing at a deeper level. Plan a team retreat for your group.

Run it yourself or enlist an outside consultant to run the retreat, so that you can participate as well.

Frosty Westering, now retired from coaching, conducted a preseason team-building outing every single year for his Pacific Lutheran University football team. He made a concerted effort to make college football fun and to facilitate strong bonding experiences for his team members. His team-first approach contributed to an impressive amount of success during his 40 years as a coach.

Frosty built in fun. He carved out time for team bonding away from the practice routine. He established a culture at Pacific Lutheran that included winning but also went beyond it. His team members enjoyed the journey. Retired UCLA softball coach Sue Enquist also took her team members on a trip away from training, to help them establish strong bonds and develop a belief in themselves as a unit.

"COMING TOGETHER IS A BEGINNING. KEEPING TOGETHER IS PROGRESS. WORKING TOGETHER IS SUCCESS."
— HENRY FORD

Enquist fostered a team-first mentality by welcoming team members into the UCLA family and being clear about what it meant to uphold that strong tradition of winning. Don't worry about being perfect, just give your all. Bring a positive attitude. Do the very best you can in the role you're in. The UCLA program was successful thanks in large part to Enquist's team-first approach.

What are your expectations for your team? How can you help your team members buy into your program? If you already have a tradition rolling, it may be a matter of convincing everyone to stay the course. Try not to get so distracted by success that you lose sight of the core principles that led you there. If you are just getting started or still trying to build a successful program, be open about sharing and explaining your philosophy. Scout out who the influential team members are, and win them over. Ask them to help you sell your team-first approach to the rest of the group. As the program continues, the veterans will likely take ownership of the responsibility to foster this mentality among the newcomers. As Ronald Nored, of the Butler Bulldogs, explains perfectly, "We have a culture here, and the culture is 'We.'"

CHALK TALK:

X EMPHASIZE THE TEAM-FIRST PHILOSOPHY REPEATEDLY. EXPLAIN HOW YOUR DECISIONS CONTRIBUTE TO THE TEAM'S OVERALL SUCCESS.

O UTILIZE THE POWER OF PUBLIC PRAISE TO REINFORCE THE VALUE OF EVERY PERSON'S CONTRIBUTION AND ROLE WITHIN YOUR TEAM.

X DO NOT BE AFRAID TO CALL OUT OR DISCIPLINE THOSE WHO FAIL TO UPHOLD THE TEAM-FIRST PHILOSOPHY.

O LOOK FOR INNOVATIVE WAYS TO BREAK THE ROUTINE AND CREATE OPPORTUNITIES FOR TEAM MEMBERS TO BOND.

PROFILES

DICK GOULD: What's Best for the Team

Dick Gould, retired men's tennis coach at Stanford University, had a saying: "Fear no one, respect everyone." "He always said that to us, and we kind of believed it," says Alex O'Brien. "My senior year, we won with a team that had absolutely no business winning." O'Brien was one of many athletes who took on the responsibility of upholding the Stanford tradition. He spoke of going to the finals, which for years was held at the University of Georgia. "I remember every year we walked into Georgia for the NCAA Tournament, we really acted like it was our home court."

At a college as renowned as Stanford, Gould also coached genuine scholars. Paul Goldstein shouldered a tough academic program, majoring in Human Biology, and at the same time became the first athlete in college tennis history to play for four NCAA team tournament champions. During Goldstein's senior year, he played number-one singles and led Stanford to a 28–0 regular season record. Gould recognized Goldstein's student-athlete achievements by saying, "I have been blessed with outstanding young people in my 36 years of coaching at the collegiate level. However, I can think of only one or maybe two players for whom I could give as high a recommendation as Paul."[1]

Goldstein's senior year, the 1998 Stanford team not only went 28–0, they lost just three team points the entire season. This remarkable achievement came about because Gould has always stressed the team over individual achievements. That's hard in a game like tennis, because a player has to develop supreme self-confidence to stand all alone out there. "It's hard to motivate six prima donnas," says former Stanford player Jim Hodges. "You want the team to win, but you want everybody to lose so you can move up the ladder. Dick always knew what was best for the team."[2] Former athletic director Ted Leland agrees. "He's a master at getting the top players in the country to consistently perform at a high level in a spot in the lineup that is best for the team." Alex O'Brien also felt that emphasis. He says Gould "taught you to respect your teammates and to get out there and give it all you have when you're playing a match for your team." As a leading singles player, he says it was "hard to get your team to respond to that."

Gould's efforts to get players to support each other was never more in evidence than in 1998. The Bryan brothers (Bob and Mike) recall a meeting with the coaches at the beginning of that season. "As the spring season was about to begin, Coach (Gould) called our top four players into his office," remembers Bob Bryan. "He said, 'Look, guys, all four of you can play number one for us this year. How do you want me to handle the lineup?'"[3]

Paul Goldstein, as captain, spoke up and said, "Hey, Coach, we're all here to win the NCAA team title, and we don't care where you play us."[4]

BRAD STEVENS

BRAD STEVENS: "Great Teams Have Great Teammates"

Brad Stevens believes in "the team." On the Butler campus, when you walk into his office, the first thing you notice is a sign with three panel photos — one is of a small group of players tightly huddled with arms around each other, the next one is a team shot of coaches and players wearing t-shirts and hats after winning a tournament, and the last is of a group of players with their hands in the air celebrating. Under the three photos reads, "Great Teams Have Great Teammates." Another sign with the same statement and different photos hangs prominently on the locker room wall.

But it's one thing to have signs with slogans just hanging on the wall. It's another to bring the slogan to life, for it to become a fiber of your team and have your team members live it and breathe it.

That's what Brad Stevens has done. And it begins with who he and his coaching staff target to bring into their program.

"The personal attention at Butler is critical," he says. "There's a reason why kids came to Butler. When they choose Butler, one of the things they like about our academic situation is they are in class sizes of 20. The biggest class they'll ever take is 30 or 40 in a lab, so you have personal attention all over campus. That's a big deal to them, and it's a big selling point for us. We can't say something and not do it. The other thing is we're values based. Every decision that we make is based on a set of core values that our program has. You can always bring it back to your core values if you are constantly talking about it and believe in something strongly enough. We have values on the wall. They are very clear. Our guys all know what they are. They know them from the time we've recruited them. It's something that we can always refer to. There's a clear expectation. The first PowerPoint slide we show them on their recruiting visit is our expectations of our players. It's not, 'I hope you come.'

"Those expectations for me are: you compete on and off the court. You believe. You believe you can beat anybody if you're doing your job or playing your role. You have to be degree seeking. If you want to go to the NBA, fine, but if you have a lockout, you'd better get your butt back in class. That's going to happen with both of our guys [Gordon Hayward, a first-round NBA draft pick of the Utah Jazz in 2010, and Shelvin Mack, a second-round NBA draft pick of the Washington Wizards in 2011]. I'm excited about that. The other one — and the most important one — is you must be a great representative of your high school in all ways, on the court and off. And with that, we look for a 'what's best for the school, what's best for the team' mentality."

Basically, Stevens and his staff target recruits who exemplify the same attitude and characteristics that Stevens did as a high school recruit and as a college student-athlete. Stevens learned and honed his ability to put the team first as a guard on head coach Bill Fenlon's basketball team about an hour's drive from the Butler campus in Indianapolis at DePauw University, located in Greencastle (Indiana). After graduating from Zionsville (Indiana) High School as the school's all-time leader in points, assists, steals, and three-point shots made, and averaging 26.8 points per game during his senior year, Stevens joined the NCAA Division III school with high hopes of continuing his basketball success, contributing to a lot of team wins while also earning a degree at the academically demanding institution. While Stevens did earn Dean's List honors and a degree in Economics, his time on the court didn't go as he envisioned.

In his four-year career, during which the team had a 56–45 record, Stevens started in only 22 of the 101 games. He went from being a big-time scorer in high school, the best player on the court during many

(continued on next page)

games in a state where high school basketball reigns supreme, to playing on a Division III college team where he averaged about seven points a game during his career.

Bill Fenlon, his college coach, believes Stevens's experience in college helped shape how he now leads the Butler Bulldogs as head coach.

"Brad was a guy who had been a big-time high school scorer and, frankly, he had expectations, we had expectations, and those things don't always work out how you think they're going to work out," says Fenlon, who completed his 20th year at DePauw in 2012. "The thing that strikes me about Brad is that even though it wasn't working out exactly the way he probably planned it, he just kept plugging. He came to work every day, and he was trying to help our team be as good as it could be."

At DePauw, the coaching staff does not give a Most Valuable Player Award. Instead they give a Coaches' Award, which is based on leadership, unselfishness, attitude, dedication, and work ethic.

"I feel like, as coaches, we're preaching 'team' all the time," Fenlon says. "We're always telling everybody that they're equal, important, and valuable. Then at the end we say, 'We were just kidding. This one guy is more valuable.' I've just never felt good about that. I've never felt like I could be talking about team for however many months you do it, trying to build the team, and then start singling guys out at the end. It never made sense to me, but we do give out one award. We give it to the guy we think is the best teammate, the guy who is making the most sacrifices, and seems to care the most about the group — the one who is doing the things we talk about all the time. Brad got that award as a senior. He's one of the most selfless, team-oriented people I've ever coached. And I think that his college experience has helped shape his coaching style today."

DON SHULA: Attention to Detail

Don Shula would transform the Miami Dolphins, but Bob Griese (with Shula in photo at left) didn't know that in the late 1960s. All he knew was that he was ready for a change.

As quarterback of the Dolphins, Griese, always having been a winner, was now losing. The Dolphins entered the NFL as an expansion team in 1966, and a year later drafted Griese, a college star at Purdue, with the fourth overall pick in the first round. He earned the starting role soon into his rookie year and went on to earn league All-Star honors during his first two years in the NFL. Still, what mattered most to Griese — winning — eluded him and his Dolphins teammates as they compiled 15 wins and 39 losses during the franchise's first four years of existence.

Then, in 1970, the change Griese was ready for came. The Dolphins hired Don Shula, who had enjoyed a successful run as head coach of the Baltimore Colts for the previous seven seasons, during which the team won 72 percent of their games. Shula led the Colts to Super Bowl III after the 1968 season. The Colts lost, confirming New York Jets quarterback Joe Namath's guarantee of his team's victory.

During Shula's first press conference announcing his hiring as the Dolphins' new head coach, Griese remembers one of his answers very clearly to this day.

"He was asked about [me], and Shula said, 'Yeah, I like that young quarterback, he's got a lot of talent and a lot of ability, but I got to get him to stay in the pocket.'"

(continued on next page)

"I was one of the first guys he called after he got the job," Griese says. "And my first words to him were, 'You hadn't looked at any of the films before you made that comment, because there was no pocket. We were losing, and there was no pocket. So I had to run for my life. Yeah, if you give me a pocket, I'd love to stay in it.'"

When Shula arrived, not only did the Dolphins offensive line not block well enough to create a pocket consistently for Griese, they didn't do many things well; hence their record.

After the NFL strike ended in 1970, Shula took control of the Dolphins and immediately shared the message that Griese believes helped build their team into champions.

"From day one when Coach Shula arrived, it was never about individuals, it was never about himself, it was always about the team," Griese says. "And because we had been losing for four years, it was a breath of fresh air when he came in, and we were ready to buy into his way of doing things."

Shula's way of doing things included four practices a day that first preseason. After all, he needed time to implement the structured and disciplined framework of his team-first approach. The Dolphins would have a walk-through in the morning, then have breakfast, followed by a morning practice. Then they'd have lunch, an afternoon practice, then dinner. After dinner, they'd have a walk-through in the evening. Shula made clear during practices and team meetings that all the effort was geared toward building a team that would be ready to compete, work together, and expect everyone's best effort at all times. After each practice and each meeting, the team would be smarter and more prepared mentally and physically. All efforts were designed to contribute to the goal of winning — this is how the team, and the coach himself, would ultimately be judged.

"No one person was bigger than what we set out to accomplish as a team," Shula says. "There were many things I tried to do that led to creating that environment. The biggest thing I insisted on was attention to detail. I just felt there was no detail too small to be ignored. I felt they were prepared for the things I would ask them to do physically."

Details. Shula and his coaching staff would drill the players on everything, from teaching an offensive lineman how to put his hand on the ground when getting set before the snap so as not to tip off whether it was a run or a pass, to the precise first step a defender was to make on a play. Shula taught it, had them practice it, correct it, and then repeat it, repeat it, repeat it.

"It started in the classroom — I would lecture on what we wanted to get done, and they were asked to write it down and take notes on everything that was said. We followed that up with films to study, and from there you went out on the practice field and did your practice, and then at night, after dinner, we tried to perfect the things we did that day. I always thought by doing that we could gain an edge on our competition. Those are all things we paid a lot of attention to.

"They were long days [during the first training camp], but we covered every aspect of the game, and those little things are what I think helped us win more than anything else. Attention to detail, everyone knowing and improving in his role, and understanding how to work together to make big things happen.

"I always felt that the team that made the fewest errors wins the game. So we'd work to address that by repetition, having them execute their assignments correctly."

Everyone was on equal footing when it came to Shula holding them accountable.

"He'd get on everybody's ass; nobody was exempt," Griese says. "Even the leaders of the team, myself, [and NFL Hall of Fame middle linebacker] Nick Buoniconti, who was strong and opinionated, and Shula would jump all over his ass if he would jump offsides or if he would be caught pass interfering. Or he'd get on my ass. Nobody was free from his criticism if they were doing something wrong that would hurt the team. Throw an interception, throw a pick, he'd get on my ass. He would get on us, but he would always make it about the thing we were doing, the pick or jumping offsides. He never made it personal.

"We can't have a tight end that's jumping offsides on the cadence, or a defensive guy jumping offsides. You have to do it the right way. If you can't do it the right way, you just can't play. If you're a running back and you fumble the football, you can't play. If you're a quarterback and you throw interceptions, you can't play. If you're an offensive lineman and you keep jumping offsides or you hold, and you get penalties all the

(continued on next page)

time, you can't play. Everybody saw that what [Shula] was saying was absolutely correct.

"When he got on me, I just thought that's good, I know he's being fair and honest and I know he's doing this for the betterment of the team. And I know if he gets on me, these other guys, when he gets on them, they're going to take it in the right way. He was an equal-opportunity guy, getting on everybody. Because he was creating a standard for how we were going to do things, how we would execute during games, and it didn't take long for that to happen."

In 1970, using that first training camp of four-a-day practices in his first year as head coach, Shula helped turn around a team that had only won 15 games the previous four seasons to ten wins in his first season. The following seasons are of NFL lore, as the Dolphins became the first team in league history to play in three consecutive Super Bowls, winning back-to-back championships in 1972 and 1973. And many of Shula's Dolphins teams were the least penalized in the NFL each season.

The 1972 team achieved a feat that had not been achieved before or since — they finished with a perfect 17–0 record, punctuated by their 14–7 Super Bowl VII win against the Washington Redskins.

The offense featured five players who would go on to be inducted into the NFL Hall of Fame: Griese, fullback Larry Csonka, wide receiver Paul Warfield, and offensive linemen Jim Langer and Larry Little. The defense, which finished as the best statistically in the NFL that season, had only one NFL Hall of Famer in Buoniconti. He was the leader of the No-Name Defense, a nickname that perfectly captured their correct, nothing flashy, make-you-earn-it style. "They didn't make mistakes," says Shula, "and they didn't give up big plays, because they were where they were supposed to be, doing what the play called for." The No-Name Defense's style epitomized Shula's coaching style, a symphony of 11 blue-collar guys each playing their role, doing their job.

"I'd like to say nothing happened by accident," Shula said. "There was always a lot of emphasis and preparation, and the big thing is making your players buy into what you are selling. You want to be excited about what you are saying and what you are asking them to do."

Once Shula became his coach with the Dolphins, it didn't take long for Csonka to become a believer.

"We went from a losing team to a winning team in the flick of a finger. That's what gave him his validity. To that point, we put up with him because we had to, to keep our jobs," Csonka says. "But then, when we started to win, we thought, 'You know what? This son of a gun is right. We started to believe in him and we started to win even more. Then we got downright obnoxious about it and started to roll on it, and smell like it, and live it. Like it was our idea too, but it was really his. He's the one that said we're going to be on the field four times a day. He said, 'When the San Francisco or Green Bay or New England teams come down to play in 85 degrees, we're going to own them in the fourth quarter.' And we did. They were dying out here in the heat. He [helped us to win] by working us out in that heat.

"He was very approachable, but he was dedicated to winning. He wasn't an emotional guy in the sense that we're going to get all fired up. It was a calmer approach. It was about strategy. While everybody else was jumping up and down and hootin' and hollerin', he was already thinking about what was going to happen on the next play and the play after that."

Of all the hundreds of men who have served as a head coaches in the NFL, Shula finished his career with more victories than any of them — 347 to be exact, 23 more wins than Chicago Bears legendary coach George Halas, and 77 more wins than the Cowboys' Tom Landry, who is third on the all-time NFL wins list.

Even with all the victories and success, Shula held true to the team-first principles he shared in that first training camp with the Dolphins in 1970.

"I had a conviction that everything we did and everything I demanded from my players was geared to making us better as a team," Shula says. "You have to have conviction in the direction you want to go, and then you have to do everything in your power to get there. Some people have convictions and visions and goals that are great in and of themselves, but they never do the things that are necessary to achieve those convictions or goals. I think that's the big thing. Also, you have to stay ahead of the competition.

"No matter how much we won, there are always things you learn along the way. You never want to feel like you have all the answers. When you start to feel that way, you find out you *don't* have them all. Somebody that might be working a little bit harder ends up with the answers."

JOHN WOODEN: Fire-testing the Team-First Approach

John Wooden didn't only teach his teams about basketball — he helped them to learn more about themselves.

The summer of 1948 was one of joyous uncertainty for George Stanich (in photo at left). He had just returned from London for his junior year at UCLA, fresh off a bronze-medal performance in the high jump at the Olympic Games. Stanich may have been a world-class Olympic athlete, but basketball remained his favorite sport. And in 1948, the methodical, slow-down strategy of former UCLA basketball coach Wilbur Johns was over.

Johns, who became the UCLA Athletic Director upon leaving the head basketball coach position, hired a young coach from Indiana State Teachers College to replace him.

He hired John Wooden.

"I didn't know who this guy was from Indiana, but I was happy to have a new coach because I knew everybody would start on the same page," Stanich says. "That first year [1947] at UCLA was difficult for me, from the academics to making enough money to eat. On top of that, I had to fight for a spot to play against these guys who were a lot older and had already established their place with Coach Johns."

Venturing to Westwood to play at UCLA was the furthest Stanich had ever been from home.

"Everybody told me, 'You shouldn't leave [Sacramento] and go down there, you're gonna get lost, it's a big city, you're not going to play,' and on and on," Stanich says. "And I tell you, coming down to UCLA was a tough time for me. I was real lonely. My studies were going bad, and I started to ask myself, *Do I really belong in the university?* I had doubt, and not a little. A lot."

John Wooden came at just the right time for George Stanich.

During those first few weeks of practice in the fall of 1948, while Wooden was teaching his style of offense and defense, Stanich was happy for a new beginning. Wooden's up-tempo, fast-break style, which he had learned as an All-American guard at Purdue in the early '30s, suited Stanich well. He felt like a caged tiger set free.

Then they played a few games, and those feelings changed.

"The second week of the season, we went up to play against St. Mary's and San Francisco. We beat them, but not by much [61–58 and 61–57, respectively]. When we came back to practice, Coach Wooden forgot about offense, he forgot about defense, he just went to work on us. Conditioning, conditioning, conditioning. I've never been so tired."

Stanich bristled at the long hours of running. Only years later, when he became a coach himself at El Camino College, did he realize the value of Wooden's strong belief in conditioning. Stanich noticed that each drill had a specific purpose. Never running just to run, but rather practicing proper cuts as Wooden stood nearby correcting mistakes. After all, Wooden explained, you never could hit somebody with a pass running straight. It is harder to defend if you hit someone cutting at an angle. Stanich believes this is one of the characteristics that made Wooden a master coach — his ability to devise drills suited to the personnel he had and to effectively teach the fundamentals in a meaningful, productive way. No wasted motion, no wasted time.

Through the sweat and fatigue, the transformation of UCLA basketball was becoming clear to Stanich. Wooden would see to it that the young men on his team would be the best-conditioned student-athletes on the West Coast. Wooden had learned to make conditioning a priority when he played for Hall of Fame Coach Ward "Piggy" Lambert at Purdue.

It was this conditioning that led to Stanich's belief that if the score was close near the end of the game, UCLA would win because they were better prepared to win.

"You know, when a kid goes through the hard work, he doesn't like it," says Stanich. "But inside, way inside, you want it and you seek it, because you know it's going to make you better. I believed in Coach Wooden, and I know that he wanted us to be the best we could become.

"And that's not just in basketball. That's in life."

George Stanich realizes this now, but in 1948 his coach's intent wasn't as clear, and his frustration and loneliness mounted.

However, over the course of their first year together at UCLA, the bond between Stanich and Wooden began to grow. Wooden saw a little bit of himself in Stanich. Wooden, like Stanich, grew up on a farm only to have his family lose it after a few bad investments. Stanich hadn't yet learned much about his coach's personal life or goals, other than how close he was to

(continued on next page)

his family and the meticulous way he planned the foundation — conditioning, fundamentals, and team spirit — for UCLA basketball. Stanich hadn't yet realized that Wooden wanted the best for him as much as he did for himself.

Then Stanich's world was shaken. His relationship with Wooden was fire-tested before becoming stronger, as his youthful pride squared off against Wooden's team-first approach.

The 6-foot-3-inch Stanich played center in a day when that usually meant being a flat-footed plodder good for rebounding, a few points, and little else. With his jumping ability and aggressiveness, Stanich was a force in the middle, averaging about nine of the 51 points UCLA averaged during his first season of 1947–48.

Early in the 1948–49 season, in an attempt to get the biggest and most athletic guys on the team in the lineup, Wooden switched Stanich from center to shooting guard. Stanich couldn't believe it. Sports had always been an escape, where he could just play and compete, undisturbed by the doubts and challenges that sometimes clouded his mind. On the pitching mound or jumping over a high-jump bar or on a basketball court, he could get away from all his personal struggles.

And now Wooden was telling him to play guard. And if he didn't like it, Wooden would make a seat available next to him on the bench.

"I really locked horns with him when he switched me to guard," Stanich recalls. "I thought that at guard, you have to work too hard. I liked grabbing rebounds and scoring close to the basket. I really struggled with it and resisted it.

"But the team was paramount to Coach, and it always came first no matter what. I really felt that moving to guard hurt me and that it maybe wouldn't forward me as a player, as far as my getting more notoriety and acclaim so I could go to the pros. You're never happy with everything, and there will always be things that are abrasive. But you learn from them."

Even up until recent years, when the two would talk, Stanich would kid Wooden about not keeping him at center. A man in his late 70s kidding his coach, who was in his 90s, about a decision he had made in 1948. "I could've been an NBA star if you just would have kept me at center," Stanich used to say to his old coach. "But nope, you got me out there handling the ball and shooting from outside. You knew I couldn't shoot worth a dang."

Lack of faith in his jump shot was part of Stanich's resistance to changing positions. He was comfortable at center. Playing guard was an unknown, and he doubted his shooting and dribbling ability, all the while knowing that he could dominate the stiffs playing center. Even his teammates were surprised at the move. "He could jump out of the dang gym, and now he's going to play farther away from the basket?" said Ralph Joeckel, Stanich's teammate from 1948–1950.

At the time, Wooden was an unknown new coach with as much to prove as Stanich. The nation would soon find out that designing a team was one of Wooden's many strengths. And he saw Stanich playing shooting guard when he put the pieces of his team together for the best fit.

"I thought that George could never be an outstanding center, but he had the quickness and unselfishness to become an outstanding guard," Wooden said. "I felt that we would have better team balance with him at guard and another person who could only play center at that position."

Wooden was right. Playing the guard position, Stanich led UCLA to back-to-back conference championships, Wooden's first two of 19 his teams won at UCLA. And in Stanich's senior year, he was selected as an All-American — the first of 24 First Team All-American selections Wooden coached at UCLA.

Wooden's first team finished with a record of 22–7, bettering Coach Johns's 12–13 team from the year before. After retiring, Wooden called his first team at UCLA one of his favorites to coach because of the acceptance by the players of a new system. This helped ease Wooden's transition to his new surroundings, which were hectic compared to his home state of Indiana. The 1949–50 season was more of the same, with the team finishing 24–7 and advancing to the national tournament for the first time in school history. The national tournament then consisted of the top eight teams in the nation. UCLA lost to Bradley in the first round. Wooden believes that team was one of three that fell short, but could have won a championship.

"At that time, I was looking for and seeking an answer to, 'What am I going to do with my life?'" Stanich says. "And I looked at Coach Wooden and the way he led us as a team. He would always do what was best for the team, and he asked for and expected the same out of us. I fought it, but deep down I was hungry for someone to push me out of what I found comfortable to a position where I could contribute to the team in the most valuable way.

"That has stuck with me to this day — put your team and your family before your own selfish desires, and always ask yourself the question, *How can I best contribute to this team?*"

BRAD STEVENS: Emphasizing Strong Bonds

Championship Teams

*"Championship teams share a moment that few
other people know. The overwhelming emotions
are derived from more than pride.
Your devotion to your teammates, the depth of your
sense of belonging, is something like blood kinship.
Rarely can words fully express it.
It is the bond that selflessness forges."*
— Bill Bradley
Sign hanging in the Butler men's basketball locker room

At no time were the overwhelming emotions more evident than in the Butler locker room in the bowels of Houston's Reliant Stadium, minutes after they lost the championship game against Connecticut in April 2011.

Butler had just completed their remarkable run that led to a second straight appearance in the NCAA championship game. A year before, they were one half-court rim-clanging shot by Gordon Hayward away from beating Duke in the championship. Against Connecticut, many shots clanged — 52 of 64 shots to be exact — on their way to shooting a championship game record-low 18.8 percent.

In the locker room, just minutes after their dismal offensive showing, sadness and disappointment froze the team. Some cried, and most sat with their heads down. Then Ronald Nored, a junior guard, stood up and began walking around the room. He hugged his teammates, told them him how much they meant to him and the team. Others followed. Teammates embraced, encouraged each other, refusing to allow the sadness of the moment to defeat the bond they'd forged throughout the season.

Nored reflected on the locker room scene after completing one of the first team weightlifting workouts in August 2011, as he prepared for the 2011–12 season, his senior year at Butler.

"We have to be a shining light for everyone else, and sometimes when we're hurting, the best thing to do is help someone else," Nored says. "I saw those guys were hurt. Those are my best friends and my teammates, and I wanted them to know that it was okay. We have each other's backs. We're still a team, we'll always be a team, and it's going to be okay.

"It was really cool, because once a few of us started going around the locker room supporting each other, everyone supported each other, and that's the way we live our lives. If one guy's doing the right thing, and if a few guys are doing the right thing, then the rest are going to follow, and we're all going to support each other. And when you do that, you build such a strong bond. That was the coolest thing for me. To this day, it's hard to see video clips of UConn celebrating or anything like that, but that moment (in the locker room) was just about everyone else, and it's always about everyone else. That's what Coach Stevens creates. I try to do everything I can to inspire someone else to be in a better position when I see them. That's something I strive to do, and that was a time for me to do that, and there was no way I could have passed up on that."

Matt Howard cried hard with a towel draped over his head when Nored grabbed him and hugged him. The floppy-haired forward had established himself as the poster child of Butler Basketball while the team performed on the national stage during the past two tournament runs. About Howard, who graduated with a 3.7 GPA in Finance, head coach Brad Stevens says, "He'll be [playing professionally] in Europe next year, and if you have a flat tire and call him, he'll try to get back and help. That's why you win. How much more talented than him are some of the guys who are going to get drafted in the [NBA] top 15? A lot more. But he's got all the makeup. His extra ten minutes of preparation that he takes to prepare for a team, plus his mind, and how hard he works every day, make him ready to play in every way."

In the locker room, a harsh reality was setting in for Howard — he would never again wear the Butler uniform and play with this team of men he considered brothers. As his teammates removed the towel hanging over his head and embraced him, Howard fully realized in that moment how his team was able to bring the Madness to March the past two years.

"Teammates came over and told you they loved you, and hugged you, and appreciated how hard you worked, and that's what our team was all about," Howard says. "We all wanted to pick each other up and not let that one loss define who we were.

"That love and respect that we all had for each other is the main reason we were able to do what we've done."

Brad Stevens sits in his office, about a month removed from the loss to UConn, and thinks back to how his message helped set the postgame scene of his team being just that — a team.

"I told them that if somebody has to go 12-for-64, I'm glad it's you guys, because you have the character to handle it," Stevens says. "That's what this

(continued on next page)

is about; you have to be able to handle some of these things and help each other through it. That's the only thing I said, and then I thanked the seniors. That's the most important thing, the people in the room.

"It's not easy to be in that locker room," Stevens continues. "It never is, because you never know when it's going to end. We knew it was going to end that night, but we didn't want it to end that way. But I think it captured what our guys are all about. They're team first. They get it."

Howard believes Stevens's message and his teammates' actions in the locker room after the championship game captured the essence of The Butler Way, a university-wide theme threaded throughout campus that emphasizes commitment, denies selfishness, accepts reality, yet seeks improvement every day while putting the team above self.

"[Coach Stevens] wasn't prepared to talk about a loss, he wasn't ready for that, he didn't expect to do that," Howard says. "Essentially, his message was, hey, as much as this hurts, I would not trade being around you guys for anything, which goes back to the value he puts on building strong relationships.

"Also, he talked about each one of us [seniors], saying what he would've done on our senior day [Stevens had an eye problem that led to him leaving the last home game of their season, and therefore missing the postgame ceremony honoring seniors Howard, Zach Hahn, Shawn Vanzant, Grant Leiendecker, and Alex Anglin]. What we always do is we give each senior a chance to talk after the last game. I really like that Coach gives us that chance. He said thank you to everybody, and we let him know how much it meant to be a part of the program and part of them.

"There was a lot of hurt; guys were really down. There were a couple of us especially who were major parts of the team, and we felt like we had maybe let everybody down. But everybody rallied around each other and supported each other and echoed Coach's message — [the game] was over, and he and all the coaches were just very happy to be a part of the team.

"Coach Stevens's message helped set that tone, and it carried through the locker room. After that, we were able to allow ourselves to savor the moment and really appreciate the bond we shared as teammates who would do anything for everyone else on this team."

FROSTY WESTERING: Breakaway

Everyone knows how that first day of football practice goes. Get your equipment, suit up, and go out there under a hot August sun to work during two-a-day practices. But what if you could go to the beach instead? Hug your teammates, hold hands, and play softball? Wait a second. What kind of crazy training idea is that?

The players at Pacific Lutheran University, located south of Tacoma in Washington state, have a simple name for it: Breakaway.

Pacific Lutheran football players are known throughout the Northwest for their hard, jarring hits. Their now-retired longtime head coach used to be a Marine drill instructor. He also is a legend. Frosty Westering is one of only ten college football coaches in history to win at least 300 games. He won three NAIA titles and one Division III title, and his teams never had a losing season. Through the years, Westering had many offers to coach from bigger schools and even NFL teams, but adhered to his longtime belief that he shared in two books (*Make the Big Time Where You Are* and *The Strange Secret of the Big Time*) that explore his unique approach. His belief is, "The big time is not a place; it's the state of your heart. It's not something you get; it's something you become." Before he retired in 2003, Westering compiled an incredible 305–96–7 overall record (.756 winning percentage) in 40 seasons as a college coach.

So what's up with the beach? The best way to start explaining this is by looking at the back of his players' jerseys. Above the number there

(continued on next page)

is no name. Each one says "Lutes." That's what the team is called. "Somebody said to me, 'Frosty, you sure have a big family,' and darn, he was right," the coach remarks. Pacific Lutheran's motto is EMAL: Every Man a Lute. Westering preached the concept of the servant warrior, the player who exists to serve and not be served. "You're part of something bigger than yourself," he said. "If you're used to being served, this isn't the place for you."[5]

Building a team starts with the summer Breakaway. "I kind of knew what [Breakaway] was, but it wasn't at all what I expected," said former offensive lineman Andrew Hersey about his first trip to the Oregon coast. "All through high school, football was different. Football was all game faces on the bus. It was just amazing to me that a football team could have so much fun together. It's just a different mentality."[6] Former PLU athletic director Paul Hoseth, once a Westering assistant, put it this way: "I've seen lots of kids who show up and wonder, 'Is this a different planet?'"[7] Westering would routinely stop practice for everything from a team Popsicle break to giving his famed "Attaway" cheer to Mount Rainier off in the distance.

Westering's coaching philosophy actually began in the Marines. He recalls, "I'm thankful for my time in the military, but I spent my entire time there thinking there's got to be a better way." He felt the same way about his days as a football player in Iowa. "I played on a lot of good teams, but it was all kick-in-the-butt coaching," he says. "I thought at the time, I'm going to coach the way I'd have liked to be coached."

Before any practices started, Westering wanted his players to engage in team building first. They would spend three pre-season practice days on Breakaway — a trip to the Oregon coast, where they would goof around on the beach, introduce freshmen to the ways of Frosty, and talk about everything but the game. No football was allowed, but the players engaged in plenty of competition. They were getting ready for the season, only in a different way. "We're gone three days. Then we go on the field Saturday for two-a-days," Westering said. "The players are just so ready to go."[8]

Westering first started the tradition back when he coached high school football. Larry Lange remembers those early days in Elkader, Iowa, in the 1950s. "It was such a great experience," he says. At that age, "you've never been out of the town. I think we went eight miles down the road to a schoolhouse. We took showers outside, and Donna [Frosty's wife] made cookies. Parents would bring the food in. He was always organized, and he always kept us going. It just taught you all about life. It was such a great experience, kind of like the Marine Corps. We thought we were Marines because he was a Marine."

The coach wanted the boys to get to know each other, to become teammates first. "That brought the whole team together," Lange continues. "That's what he does when he has those Breakaways. Guys get so close together and nobody ever wants to get out of line because everyone buys into his program."

Westering also wanted to welcome newcomers to his brand of football. "New players are just amazed that the guys are so friendly toward them." He wanted his upperclassmen to "welcome the new guys. You don't put them down and abuse them and all that initiation stuff, which supposedly is funny. We get up on chairs and sing, but everybody does. The seniors, the coaches, we all do, and it isn't punishment for the new guys. [They] get up there, and everybody sings along with them." At Breakaway, "we're teaching this team building in a lot of different ways to start to feel good about being together."

The days on the beach would consist of different types of unusual sports: swimming relays, hustle ball, racing to build human pyramids. The players were divided into ten-man teams. That way they could get to know each other, which to Frosty was as important as the competition.

They played five-shot, a team basketball shooting contest. One competition featured a football — but the quarterbacks weren't allowed to throw. The most they could do was play receiver in blind-man football. In that game, the thrower was first blindfolded and then snapped the ball. He must throw it to the person snapping, only beyond a line about ten yards away. "That blind-man football relay is the goofiest thing," Westering recalls with a smile.[9]

The days featured constant cheers, known as Attaways. A typical back-and-forth chant with his players would run like this:

Frosty: "Hey, Lutes."
Players: "HEY, LUTES!"
"Go Lutes."
"GO LUTES!"
"Attaway."
"ATTAWAY!"

(continued on next page)

Then the team whistles and claps, screaming out cries of encouragement. In the evening they would have skit competitions and songs. Around midnight, a snack of fruit and peanut butter sandwiches was served. One evening a shy player was egged on to sing Billy Joel's "Piano Man." Although he stumbled over some of the words, he did all right. When it was over, 80 teammates started clapping and yelling. They stood up and arched their arms over their heads in big O's. That means a standing O-vation.[10]

What this adds up to is an emphasis on the team first. Westering talks about the way most coaches treat their players. "[They] motivate with fear and incentives, but criticism is the main thing — they play the put-down game. The competition [for players] is with each other for a place on the team. They're in the mirror room, which is all about me." "[Other] coaches and game plans are pretty rigid, and the players don't have much input at all. They play not to lose. They play by the book, and they have a low priority on feedback. That's the authoritarian style of a just-win-baby coach." That didn't interest Westering at all. His process was about building self-belief and allowing his players the freedom to be themselves. "Our style was believe, achieve, and succeed. You have to learn to believe in yourself and each other. We need to achieve certain goals, and the by-product was: we succeed."

Back on the beach the next day, the team would engage in a drill that had players throwing footballs across the sand at other players. It's like dodgeball, only they throw at the feet. That wouldn't stop these guys from firing off strikes. Another crazy game took place at the edge of the surf. A player from each team put his forehead on the top of a pole, and he turned around and around and around until he got dizzy — while the other nine guys of his crew were urging him to whirl "Faster! Faster!"

These were games, but they were being played rough-and-tumble, just like football. Westering felt that carried over onto the football field. He has a saying about the way he expected his team to play: "Remember, hit or be hit." Ted Riddall, an All-American lineback, explained what that meant during a game. "Because we have no fear of losing, we are able to give a total release. We play hard and try to give absolutely our best. We're in sync. Sooner or later, everyone in the program locks on to Frosty's idea of being a servant warrior."[11]

Frosty was not interested in becoming a football factory, turning out players that would go on to the NFL. At a Division III school, he knew that hardly any of his players would turn pro after their college days were over. So why should he make the season an endurance race? One of his players, defensive tackle Tyler Morrison had this to say: "When you're not going to play football after college, why not play somewhere you won't hate it every day?"[12]

At the end of Breakaway, Pacific Lutheran would get down to business — being a team that was always greater than the sum of its parts. Looking back, Westering says, "I guess I felt that you could really love this game in a way that you could teach it so people could feel good about themselves whether they won or lost on the scoreboard — as long as they gave you everything they had."

Frosty Westering's teams believed in themselves. That's why, for 40 years, they never had a losing season.

SUE ENQUIST: A "Family" Tradition

Sue Enquist helped UCLA win national softball championships as a player (one), an assistant coach (four), and as head coach (six). Every year as head coach, the preseason had one constant: an overnight trip to her childhood home on the beach in San Clemente to visit her parents, Bill and Jane, affectionately known as "Slap" and "Mama E" within the UCLA softball family. She saw this annual trip away from campus as a vital time for her team to learn more about each other as people, and to work together to accomplish challenges that may even seem impossible.

The challenge posed by Enquist during the trip in the fall of 1998 was that, while all 18 players remained on a beach towel and in physical contact the entire time, the team must work together to move the towel through three boxes drawn in the beach sand. The first box the team had to move the towel through represented the fall preseason. The second box represented the Pac-10 conference season. And the third, NCAA postseason play. Enquist shared the rules and the goal, then took a seat on the beach. Julie Adams looked at the beach towel and thought, "No way we're going to get all 18 of us on there." Impossible task. At least that was what Adams first remembered when she recalled her favorite memory from all her team trips to head coach Enquist's parents' home.

"We just started stacking each other up on our shoulders, holding each other," says Adams, an All-American third baseman at UCLA. "We were inchworming it with our toes. We were trying to figure out who could lift who up on their shoulders, who had really good balance, and could stand on one leg. Then, we finally worked together and got it done! We dog piled each other. We were so ecstatic, we figured it out, and we accomplished it."

That moment helped build the chemistry of the team that would end their season in the final game of the College Softball World Series in Oklahoma City.

"We hung that beach towel in the dugout during the entire world series," says Adams, who earned Most Outstanding Player of the College World Series honors even after dislocating her nonthrowing shoulder in the first game of the tournament. "That towel represented to us what we could accomplish when we worked together, no matter how impossible the challenge seemed."

UCLA won the 1999 National Championship 3–2 against Washington. The beach towel is an example of what Enquist hoped to get out of each preseason trip to her parents' home.

"It was about kids getting to know each other outside the ball field, because that does help to make a stronger team," Enquist says. "I always tell my student-athletes, if you don't have [that closeness], that doesn't mean you can't win. You can still win if a team doesn't love each other. But if we have a team that loves each other, you are at a huge advantage. You're at a huge advantage because the ability to make it through the tough times is even easier because you really care about one another. The real key in those team-bonding moments is to learn about how people came to be at UCLA. What are their influences, and what do they value? The answers may be different for each person, and so it opens up everybody's eyes. Being together at the beach helps everyone understand each other better and work together to become the best team we could be."

Christie Ambrosi, who, Adams points out, was key to accomplishing the beach-towel task because of her incredible ability to balance on the corner of the towel and remain on one leg as they inched the towel along the sand, found more than just fun times during the team trips to the beach. She found a family.

"We'd all be on the floor like at a slumber party, and it was just fun. It really is like family," says Ambrosi, an All-American on the 1999 national championship team. "[Enquist] didn't just incorporate the team into the trip, she let us into her family. Think about that — what sends a message more clearly than saying you, my players, are my family, and we're going to stay with my parents overnight because all of you are a part this larger family and we're all in it together.

"I was really far away from home [in Kansas]. I had no family out there. And she really took me under her wing and made sure that I felt at home, and if I ever needed anything I could always count on her. And I could. She was one of those people I could always count on. She could have just made it about softball, and some coaches would have. But she took me in and really made sure that I felt and knew that UCLA was my family away from home."

Enquist helped build the strongest of family traditions. As a member of UCLA's first national championship team, she was the first player to earn All-

(continued on next page)

American honors as a softball student-athlete at UCLA — a count that totaled 97 All-Americans in program history entering the 2011–12 season. After playing for head coach Sharon Backus, Enquist served as Backus's assistant coach for nine seasons (1980–88), then as cohead coach alongside Backus (1989–96), and then, after Backus's retirement, as head coach from 1997–2006. During her 27 years (which includes her years as a player and coach), her teams amassed 1,314 wins, an average of about 49 wins a season. She epitomized the unmatched tradition and excellence of UCLA softball. She also revered that tradition and made sure all of her players knew where they were and what the expectations were.

"A big part of your freshman year is learning the tradition," Adams says. "When you walk through the gates of Easton Stadium your freshman year, you learn the history — you learn about the people who walked before you, the people who walk with you, and when you're done, you learn about the people who walk after you. If you didn't win the National Championship at the end of the year, it wasn't the coaches who made you feel bad. As a player, you made yourself look back at the season and see what you needed to do better. That's the Bruin family, the Bruin way. And as Coach Enquist shares the tradition, it's understood that there is nobody in the program who is bigger than the four letters on the chest. As a team, you knew that. That's why we've never had names on the back of the jerseys. Because it's not about the individual, it's about the letters on the front of the chest; it's about what nobody has across the country — and that's our tradition."

Given the winning tradition of UCLA softball, Enquist's challenge was not recruiting the top talent in the country to come to UCLA. The challenge was taking the top young softball players in the country and molding them into the best college softball team in the country.

"The first thing I knew I had to do was deprogram them from thinking they had to be perfect, because every softball girl's dream is to be a Bruin," Enquist says. "There are very few softball programs in the country that have a sustainable excellence. For the majority of student-athletes we recruited, it was a dream to be there, and because of that they want to be perfect. I'm only going to demand two things: that you give me 100 percent of what you have every day, and that you stay positive. It clicked with people who realized I never said they had to hit .300. There were going to be people it didn't click with right away, because they came from programs where there was a double standard — people who said, 'I'm so good I don't have to show up on Monday through Friday.'

"I was the coach that would say run if a pitcher was slacking off in the bullpen. I was the coach that made everybody run if the best player went 4-for-4 and had a crappy attitude. People who understood that knew it was very easy to play for me. I told them point-blank, 'I already trust you. I'm not the coach that's going to say you have to earn my trust. I already trust you. I picked you out of a thousand kids. I believe in you, and we're going to go out and win together. If, in your effort and attitude, you show any doubt I was wrong, I will treat you like a kindergartner. I will push you and take away that trust until you build it back up.' I think that's where I was able to do something very fundamental. Own your mistakes. *So,* people thought, *'she's letting me go for it. She's letting me fail. She just said own it.'* No one gets stuck in it, and I think that's why it worked for a majority of the kids, and that's why it was so fun for everybody."

Christie Ambrosi believes that's the genius of Enquist.

"There was a rich tradition, and you feel obligated to respect that," Ambrosi says. "[Enquist] drilled it in us, that the only thing that you can control is yourself, and within that is your effort and your attitude. So with that, she takes all of us and our different personalities who were all big fish in the little pond, and now we're little fish in the big pond. And she was able to manipulate the situation so that we all were unselfish and just became a part of this tradition. First thing was introducing us to the tradition of UCLA softball, all the wins, all the players who came before us. Then, it was talking about the letters on the front of our chest.

"Now, when we got there, we thought we were really good players, and we *were* really good. But she really did break us out of that mindset, so there wasn't a feeling of, 'Oh, it's about me, I want to be a superstar.' There was none of that. We all just wanted to keep that tradition going. She really did break us down and build us back up to be stronger as individuals and as a team when we got to UCLA."

BRAD STEVENS: The Culture of "We"

Brad Stevens works to cultivate a team-first culture. Ronald Nored, who teammates describe as the vocal leader of both NCAA Final Four teams, believes that because of this, Butler basketball will continue to breed the same type of togetherness that leads to sustained achievement.

"I think when it comes down to it, the reason I came here was to be successful," Nored says. "Like any college freshman, you want to come in and start. You want to come in and play a lot of minutes, but when I got here, although I did start every game up until last year, that didn't become the important thing to me anymore. It really was about success and being around Coach Stevens and knowing what he values. He instilled that in all of us."

It's worth repeating what Nored said previously: "We have a culture here, and the culture is 'We.' With the guys Butler has been known to recruit, it's really easy for us to buy into that, because that is the type of people we are. Those are the kind of backgrounds we grew up in, and the coaches do a really good job of not only finding really good players, but finding really good players that are going to buy into that. We have a culture here that buys into 'team.' So, whatever we do, if it's academics and making sure our grades are right, we have team goals for that. We have team goals in the weight room, too. What we do buys into the team picture that's bigger than yourselves. You aren't receiving good grades for yourself. You aren't lifting weights for yourself. You are doing it so we can reach our team goals, and that goes into what we do on the floor. You're not scoring just for yourself. You're not being a great defensive player or rebounder for yourself. That's something you are sacrificing for the betterment of our team. We really believe that if everyone does what they are supposed to do, if everyone does their job, we're putting ourselves in a position to be successful — whether that's going to win a National Championship, a Horizon League Championship, or however we define success in a season. You doing your job is putting us in a better position to be successful, and that's just something we kind of live. That's something the guys before us lived and we got to watch the guys older than us do it, so now it's just about that trickling down. That's something we need to instill in all of our new freshmen every year, for us to continue to succeed the way we have been.

"I think the first thing we do is our summer goals. When they come here over the summer, we have a certain GPA to achieve, and it's like, *All right, this isn't about you. You can mess this up or help us out.* So you have to buy into that. Then, if you hold yourself accountable, we can be more successful and have a better chance to do good things. I think it just comes from discipline and us older guys showing what we value. We love hanging out in our locker room, and we don't talk about that every single day, but we live it every single day. The freshmen have to see the way we live and see how this program operates. If they follow the older guys, that's good, and if they don't, then we let them know there's things we can do better. There are things they can do better. Coach Stevens sets the expectation and sets the standard, and we take on the responsibility of making sure it doesn't slip."

Gordon Hayward, whose last shot at Butler nearly made them national champions in 2010 and is now a member of the Utah Jazz, may sum up the Butler team-first approach most succinctly.

"We never thought about scoring the most, or getting the most attention," Hayward says. "What sets Butler apart is we take as much pride in setting a screen so a teammate can hit a shot as we would hitting a shot. We take as much pride putting a body on a defender so a teammate can grab a rebound. We do the little things that lead to big things. And if the team is successful, then we're all successful. Coach Stevens reminded us of that every day."

Chapter 5

MOTIVATING AND INSPIRING YOUR TEAM

"IF YOUR ACTIONS INSPIRE OTHERS TO DREAM MORE, LEARN MORE,
DO MORE, AND BECOME MORE, YOU ARE A LEADER."
— JOHN QUINCY ADAMS

When it's game time, you have an incredibly important job to do. I'm not talking about choosing a lineup, designing a strategy, or calling plays — your job goes beyond that. Whether you are pacing the sideline or running the boardroom, you need to be a master motivator. You are responsible for ensuring that you are pulling the absolute best effort out of each of your team members. And sure, all of your team members will be influenced by their own motivational strategies and the extent to which they want to — and believe they can — turn in an optimal performance. But each and every one of them will also look to you for an external boost. This goes beyond a well-prepared pep talk. If you are in charge of helping a group of people attain success through maximum effort, you need a clear understanding of how to motivate others. Often, that understanding is exactly what helps outstanding coaches and executives rise above the fray.

What motivates people to perform their best? The coaches featured in this book have unlocked the secret. They've used a wide variety of methods to inspire their athletes and teams to achieve greatness — from holding team retreats to handing out praise when adversity strikes to demanding exceptional effort on a daily basis and publicly posting progress. One resounding theme is the individualized approach. Championship coaches recognize that what motivates one team member may not work for another team member. They tailor their motivational strategies to match the individual's needs.

One season removed from a national championship, then Notre Dame head coach Lou Holtz seized a motivational moment, to prevent complacency among his upperclassmen and to encourage a brand-new freshman on the team to step up.

Notre Dame had won the national championship in 1988, which meant that many of Lake Dawson's teammates had experienced the pinnacle of success. Coach Holtz pointed out Dawson's breakout performance at freshman camp and challenged the upperclassmen — a season removed from a national championship — to be like Dawson. "Coach Holtz said you don't talk about being a national champion," Dawson reflects, "you do the things that make you a national champion. You practice, you study, you work hard, you win each game play by play. You don't look toward the next game, you just take care of the first game, and then the next game, you wake up and you're in the bowl game, you're a national champion. You don't just talk about it, you put the words into action. Looking back on that team meeting, that one moment had a tremendous impact in motivating me and the whole team to practice and give the effort every day it takes to become a national champion."

Holtz understood his upperclassmen well enough to know that introducing a new freshman at the first team meeting would light a fire under them. When you are in charge of a group of people, take the time to gather information about your team members. Find out what makes each person tick. Why did they get involved in the first place? What keeps them hanging around? What inspires them to give their all, even when no one is watching? Spend time observing your team with these questions in mind. Talk to your team members about these things. Consider bringing in a consultant to do personality testing with your team; results from these assessments shouldn't be thought of as definitive, but rather they can provide grist for the mill, particularly regarding how to best communicate with various team members and what kind of role individuals can play to help create a motivational climate. Another method of gaining insight about your personnel is to administer a survey to your team members. It can be as simple as passing out index cards and asking each person to answer a couple of questions, such as "What do you enjoy about this sport/job/team?" and "What motivates you to perform your best?" When you are in charge, do the best you can to find out what drives each person to give his or her all. Former Stanford tennis coach Dick Gould, who led his student-athletes to 17 team national titles, ten singles national titles, and seven doubles national titles, was extremely adept at getting the best out of each person on his team by knowing which buttons to push and doing that at just the right time.

Some people are motivated by a strong fear of failure. Unfortunately, this can also hinder people from performing their best. Someone who fears failure may become tentative in the face of adversity, hesitating to act in order to avoid making a mistake. How you talk to these folks is paramount. They are their own worst critic, and providing additional criticism may simply cause them to shut down. If you as a coach are constantly pulling them out of the game as soon as they make an error, you are probably contributing to the culture of fear that exists in their heads. This will lead to hesitant performance at best, and a performance meltdown at worst.

To bring the best out in these individuals, help them recognize that their mistake was not the end of the world, point out that they have the power to make adjustments, and instill confidence that they will be able to change things for the better in the future. How they perceive failure will be a key to determining their future effort and persistence. Therefore, how you define their mistakes is very important. Through your words, you can assist them in attributing failure to external factors they can't control, like the referees or the weather, which can enhance their motivation, or internal factors, which they can improve through hard work and adjustments. When individuals who fear failure experience success, remind them to be sure to attribute their success to their own talents and effort. Point out specifically how their performance contributed to the team's success. This will enable them to continue to work hard with the belief that their efforts will lead to further achievement in the future.

Stanford's Gould was a master at this. Gould provided just the right kind of motivation for Alex O'Brien, who won the 1992 NCAA Division I National Championship in singles and doubles and helped bring home the team national championship victory as well that year. Because Gould knew that O'Brien was enormously self-critical, he provided a heavy dose of encouragement, even when O'Brien struggled with opponents.

Many people are highly motivated by encouragement. While some leaders in sports and business may believe that punishment is the way to shape behavior, there is actually a good deal of research supporting the idea that positive reinforcement works more effectively to get people to act in the way you desire. It comes down to basic psychology: reward the behaviors that you want to occur more frequently. When you see your team members working extra hard, getting something right after several tries, or overcoming adversity, find a way to reinforce the behavior. Tom Osborne, former Nebraska football coach turned athletics director, was a big believer in this.

"REALLY GREAT PEOPLE MAKE YOU FEEL THAT YOU, TOO, CAN BECOME GREAT."
— MARK TWAIN

There are a variety of effective methods for rewarding behavior that you want to see your team members repeat. Dole out words of praise, give them time off to rest, bring food, offer a raise, or provide them with the right to choose the last activity of the day. Or select a fun activity yourself to end the day on. An example of this is illustrated by New England Patriots three-time Super Bowl–winning head coach Bill Belichick, who, during training camps, has traditionally picked an offensive or defensive lineman to catch a punt at the end of practice — imagine a 300-pound man staggering under a sky-high punt, settling underneath it, and then cradling the ball in his massive arms as his teammates burst into excited cheers. You might be surprised how far a simple reward like this will go towards motivating your team members.

Incorporating enjoyable assignments as a reward can serve a dual purpose; activities like the one described above may also fulfill the valuable function of reminding your team that what they're doing is fun. Sometimes our efforts to achieve can be exhausting. At those times, it may be difficult for team members and even coaches to remember *why* we're doing what we're doing. The motivational atmosphere can become depleted. As a coach or leader of your team, it is important to recognize this downshift in energy and find a way to recharge your team's batteries. This might be through some much-needed rest and time off. It may also be an opportunity to do something fun as a team. Change the scenery or alter the routine, and build in an activity that lightens the mood and energizes the group.

Some individuals will be motivated by clear guidelines for achievement. These are your high achievers who are also very detail oriented. If you give them a checklist for how to attain a certain measure of success, you will find them hard at work every day on each of those checklist items, laboring consistently towards the goal. For these folks, it can be highly motivating not only to have a checklist, but to see those items checked off. Consider the star-sticker chart you may have had in grade school to provide encouragement and to denote success, but that also highlighted the areas that needed improvement. This is a rudimentary version of what Coach Anson Dorrance of University of North Carolina women's soccer acclaim is well known for — the Competitive Cauldron. The Competitive Cauldron is a method Dorrance uses to give each member of his team something to strive for. Every practice drill is scored. Each player is evaluated on every single thing they do in practice every single day. And the results are tallied and posted publicly on a regular basis, for the entire team to see. If you want to earn a starting spot on the UNC roster and you see your name towards the bottom of that chart, you know you've got your work cut out for you. And there's no one to blame but yourself. Motivation? Dorrance has it figured out.

If you have laid the groundwork by sending the message to your team that you care about them as people, they will already feel valued by you. They will want to please you. They will crave positive words from you, and in order to receive them, they will do as you ask. By understanding motivational concepts, you can create a highly supportive environment that provides team members with ample opportunities to learn, fosters their desire to work hard, encourages them to recover and grow from mistakes, and inspires them to achieve their individual and team goals.

"ANY MAN CAN WIN WHEN THINGS GO HIS WAY; IT'S THE MAN WHO OVERCOMES ADVERSITY THAT IS THE TRUE CHAMPION."
— JOCK EWING

When adversity arises — and if you wait long enough, it definitely will arise! — you want to be able to rally the troops. It is nearly impossible to do this if you yourself are feeling defeated. So step one is to recognize your own negative attitude and lack of belief in your team, and then counter that. What has your team shown you in the past when things got tough? Can you think back to a time when they rose to the challenge? History is littered with underdog victories and come-from-behind stories, right? So why can't your team join those ranks? It's possible, but only if you believe it's possible. Once you've convinced yourself of this, leave your defeatist mindset behind and start thinking clearly about strategy. Because your team needs two things at this point: instruction and confidence. They will look to you as their leader, and they need you to give them information about how to perform their best and get the job done. They also need to see that you think they can do it. As Lou Holtz likes to say, "Things are never as good as you think they are, and they're never as bad as you think they are." Holtz tells a story about a football game his team was losing by 31 points when they broke for the half. In the locker room at halftime, he did some fast math and reminded the team that they typically averaged 34 points a game, which meant 17 points a half. With those 17 points, plus two touchdowns that could be achieved with improved defense, the game would be tied. He instilled confidence and said, "Now let's go do this." Find a way to help your team believe in the possibilities, and show them *how* they can make it happen.

One of the hardest concepts to both understand and implement when it comes to motivating others is this: focus on the process rather than the outcome. Winning is obviously a desired outcome. But at the end of the day, you cannot control what the competitors are going to do. What you *can* do, however, is bring your very best effort every single day. Legendary UCLA men's basketball coach John

COACHING WISDOM

"[O]ne of the things that I read in one of John Wooden's early books that resonated with me was that he mentioned that he never talked about winning to his players. I thought that was really odd. Here's a person who, in many ways, has won more than anyone, and he never talked about winning. He continually talked about the process — how you put your socks on, how you shoot a free throw, how you bend your knees, how you pass — the fundamentals and the daily things that you do that eventually lead to either winning or losing. I began to incorporate that. After reading that, I don't know that I ever talked to my players about winning. We talked about how you did things. It was more about the process than the final result."
— Tom Osborne

Wooden never talked about winning. Never. Instead, he talked about getting the details right. Everything from how to tie your shoes properly to the importance of acknowledging a teammate's assist. He believed that if you continually focus on the process, the outcome will take care of itself. NFL Hall of Fame Coach Don Shula, who won more games than any other coach in NFL history, was a huge proponent of focusing on the details. In fact, during his first season with the Miami Dolphins, he held four practices a day so that the team was engrossed in relearning the fundamentals. Instruct your team members on the correct technique, and drill them until the process becomes automatic. How does this relate to motivation? It's simple. If you are allowing your team members to concentrate on the key controllable — namely, their effort — they will improve on skills and technique, and this will help you attain your desired outcome. Positively reinforce their effort, and they'll continue to bring their best for you every single time. This is how they'll get better. This is how your team will win.

Tom Osborne shaped his approach to coaching football at Nebraska in part by adopting John Wooden's focus on the process. "I would have to say that one of the things that I read in one of John Wooden's early books that resonated with me was that he mentioned that he never talked about winning to his players. I thought that was really odd. Here's a person who, in many ways, has won more than anyone, and he never talked about winning. He continually talked about the process — how you put your socks on, how you shoot a free throw, how you

COACHING WISDOM

"Bad habits are like a good bed: easy to get into but difficult to get out of."

— Dan Gable

bend your knees, how you pass — the fundamentals and the daily things that you do that eventually lead to either winning or losing. I began to incorporate that. After reading that, I don't know that I ever talked to my players about winning. We talked about how you did things. It was more about the process than the final result."

People are thirsty for someone to follow. In general, we look for someone to lead the way. When you have a number of individuals who are looking to you to lead, you want to be sure you're providing a trustworthy model of behavior. Osborne did this at Nebraska by inspiring his players through his genuine care for them as people, his desire to help them be the best they could be, and his consistent commitment to the cause. And while we're on the topic of inspirational coaches, former University of Iowa wrestling coach Dan Gable is among the all-time best. Wrestling is a daily grind. The sport truly harkens back to the days of old when conflicts were determined by hand-to-hand combat. It is an all-consuming, physically exhausting, and mentally demanding endeavor that you absolutely have to love in order to even participate, let alone succeed. Gable, an Olympic gold medalist and a two-time national champion who went 117–1 as a wrestler at Iowa State, wrestled his team members during practice to help physically and mentally prepare them for the rigors of competition. His zeal for the sport and his willingness to put himself on the line every day for his team helped keep his team members' passion ignited. Gable expected a lot, and he gave even more. Pause for a moment and reflect on how you can demonstrate your commitment to the cause. How can you show the team your hunger to help them become the very best they can be? As a leader, what are you willing to sacrifice for your team? You can provide the motivational spark your team needs just by sharing your love of the game and being willing to go above and beyond.

Dan Gable had unparalleled passion, and it rubbed off on the men who wrestled for him. Gable also paid attention to individuals and found ways to motivate each person. Championship coaches have figured out how to inspire their team members to greatness, and they do it exceptionally well. If you understand the principles of motivation, you can do it, too.

CHALK TALK:

X PEOPLE ARE MOTIVATED IN MANY DIFFERENT WAYS. GATHER INFORMATION ABOUT HOW INDIVIDUALS ON THE TEAM MAY RESPOND TO A VARIETY OF MOTIVATIONAL STYLES.

O HELP TEAM MEMBERS ATTRIBUTE SUCCESS TO THEIR OWN TALENTS, SKILLS, AND EFFORT. HELP THEM ATTRIBUTE FAILURE TO OUTSIDE FACTORS, OR TO INTERNAL FACTORS THEY CAN CONTROL AND IMPROVE.

X PROVIDE FREQUENT REINFORCEMENT—ESPECIALLY VERBAL PRAISE — FOR THE BEHAVIORS YOU WANT YOUR TEAM TO REPEAT.

O INCORPORATE REWARDS SUCH AS REST FROM WORK OR FUN ACTIVITIES TO RENEW ENERGY AND LIGHTEN THE MOOD.

X CREATE A CONCRETE, OBJECTIVE METHOD FOR TRACKING PERFORMANCE, AND POST THE RESULTS FOR THE TEAM TO SEE.

O IN TIMES OF ADVERSITY, GIVE YOUR TEAM MEMBERS INSTRUCTIONS ON OVERCOMING OBSTACLES AND INSTILL CONFIDENCE THAT THIS IS POSSIBLE.

X FOCUS ON THE PROCESS RATHER THAN THE OUTCOME. TAKE CARE OF THE DETAILS AND TRUST THAT WINNING WILL FOLLOW.

O DEMONSTRATE YOUR PASSION AND COMMITMENT TO SACRIFICE FOR THE GOOD OF THE TEAM.

PROFILES

DICK GOULD: A Flexible Approach

In the world of college tennis, Dick Gould created a legend that may never be surpassed. He was the men's head coach at Stanford University for 38 years, and during those nearly four decades he amassed an awesome 776–148 record, for a winning percentage of .840. Featuring such players as John McEnroe, Roscoe Tanner, and the Bryan brothers, his teams won 17 NCAA team championships, going 89–10 in tournament competition since the format change in 1977. He also holds one record he particularly relishes. "When you talk about success at the end of the year," he says, "I'm very proud that everybody who played for me for four years had at least one championship ring."

In all of sports, tennis stands out as a contest of wills. A singles player has no one else to pick up the slack. He has no one else to help turn around the momentum when it starts going bad. That means a player has to go in with supreme self-confidence and maintain it throughout the ups and down of a match. How did Dick Gould help so many different individuals to become stars?

He doesn't have a set formula that he teaches all players. When asked how he has been so successful, he says, "I don't have a road map to success, but I think a key thing for me is flexibility. I was able to be flexible with different individuals and different teams."

Adapting to each player meant pushing different buttons to see how they would respond. "I can't tell you what the players think or what worked for them. They might all have different stories. Some might say I had no influence," he says, smiling. Yet, he got to know all of them very well during the year. "You're with these guys three hours-plus every day, six days a week. Stressed times — more relaxed times, you really get to know a group of ten or 12 people very, very well over a four-year period."

That close attention to his players really paid off. Alex O'Brien, who in 1992 became the first man since 1974 to win both the singles and doubles NCAA championships, remembers how each player was treated. "He had this magical way of motivating each guy and knowing how to push each guy to do his best. I remember so many of his postmatch talks. He'd go through and treat each guy completely differently."

DICK GOULD

LOU HOLTZ: Conquering Complacency

Lou Holtz said, "Lake Dawson, stand up," to his freshman wide receiver, who was sitting in the back row of an auditorium filled with his 1990 Notre Dame football teammates. The freshmen had just finished up practices as a group, and this was the first meeting for the entire team together.

Coach Holtz (pictured in photo at left with #87, Lake Dawson) said to the team: "This young man, Lake Dawson, understands what we're trying to do. We're trying to win a national championship. You want to know what it takes to be a national champion and how to practice, watch the way he practices."

Dawson was surprised by being singled out in his first meeting with his teammates.

"It was very intimidating, I'm not going to lie," Dawson says, laughing. "The way he had the room set up. I'm sitting in the back with the freshmen. All the seniors and upperclassmen are sitting in the front. So when he said, 'Lake Dawson, stand up,' [and] I stand up, all these guys turn around and look at me. All eyes are on me. And I'm talking about guys like [All-Americans] Chris Zorich and Rocket Ismail.

"Just the week before I'll never forget Ricky Watters coming out to the freshman practice, standing on the sidelines with no shirt on, gold chains, ripped up, just standing there watching us practice. And we were all like, 'Who's that guy?' and he didn't say anything, just watched for a while and walked away." (Watters was a running back who went on to become the 20th leading rusher in NFL history).

"So," Dawson continues, "I'm in this room, as a freshman, with some of the best college football players in the country, we're preseason number one in the rankings, and Coach Holtz points me out as setting the standard for work ethic. It was a lot of pressure on me, because after he said that, people wanted to chokeslam me in practice. But it also put pressure on me to see if I was going to step up or not."

He did, earning significant playing time his freshman year, which ended with the team finishing 9–3 and ranked sixth in the country. Dawson thinks that first team meeting helped to shake the team out of believing all the hype about being preseason number one and feeling the complacency that can come when praise is heaped on by the media.

"[Coach Holtz] singling me out like that was huge motivation," Dawson says. "It was big for me, and it was big for other players in the room. You had these upperclassmen like Ricky Watters, Chris Zorich, Rick Mirer, Rocket Ismail, and Tony Brooks, they're all there. And then there's me, who Coach Holtz looked at as this hard-working freshman. Not that he was looking for me to contribute or play, but he didn't want those guys to have big heads. Which, when you're coming into the season ranked number one, it's just going to happen.

"So I think that was one way of motivating those upperclassmen, by saying, 'Look, this young kid from Seattle, Washington, is busting his behind and practicing like he wants a national championship. You guys are the upperclassmen; don't let him outshine you. You know what it takes to be a national champion.'"

TOM OSBORNE: Using Positive Reinforcement

Tom Osborne, who took a more professorial approach as a coach at Nebraska (he holds both a master's and a doctorate degree in educational psychology), was ever the intense competitor. You don't win 84 percent of the games you've coached by not being an intense competitor. Osborne saw the key to coaching and teaching his players as a simple one.

"So often, coaches coach in the way they were coached, because that's all they've known," says Osborne, who, after retiring from coaching in 1997, represented the state of Nebraska by serving three terms in the U.S. House of Representatives, then after a campaign to become governor, became Nebraska's athletic director in 2007.

He says, "Some of my approach to coaching goes back to my graduate work. I was in educational psychology and looked at learning theory quite a bit. It seemed that the research pointed to the fact that the best way to change behavior was to catch somebody doing something right and to positively reinforce it, rather than always criticizing or looking for something that they're doing wrong.

"So often coaching is equated with criticizing or finding people making mistakes and harping on those mistakes. I felt that it was probably more beneficial to the performance to be positive, to try to reinforce the behavior you were looking for. It didn't mean you ignored mistakes or you tolerated a lack of effort or bad behavior, but you didn't attack the person in a personal way. In other words, sometimes coaching denigrates [and] attacks the persona or the character of the person. When that happens, the person oftentimes becomes defensive. They throw up their defenses in order to protect themselves, and sometimes they aren't even able to hear objectively what you are saying. I felt that even if you corrected a player, you let him know that you're doing it in his best interest, [that] you care about him. You could be very demanding and have very intense effort from players if they felt that what you were asking them to do was in their best interest and if, underneath it all, you cared about them as people. I felt that was important, and I think they can sense very quickly whether you genuinely care about them or whether you're putting on a front. I think it's important to be authentic."

Authentic is exactly the word All-American quarterback Steve Taylor would use to describe his college coach.

"That's the great thing about Coach — he's been the same person since day one," Taylor says. "He's been a great coach and won a lot of games, but what I like about him is you feel like you have a special relationship with him. Every player feels that way. It was your character, your effort, and your integrity that he cared about. He said as long as you do that, you're going to win more than your fair share of ball games. It's the same thing with life. You're going to have some failures, but be consistent in what you do and give 100 percent effort. Eventually, you will be successful. That's why it was never a question of *if* [Osborne] was going to win a National Championship, it was when and how many. You knew eventually it was going to happen."

As an assistant coach, Osborne had helped Nebraska win back-to-back national championships in 1970 and 1971 under head coach Bob Devaney. He finally collected his own national championship as Nebraska's head coach in 1994, followed closely by two more in 1995 and 1997. All that training in educational psychology paid off!

ANSON DORRANCE: ON THE ART OF MOTIVATION

A true motivator knows how to use psychology. In order to make it work, a coach needs to understand his players. No one has mastered this art better than Anson Dorrance {in photo at left with Cat Reddick Whitehill), the winningest coach in college women's soccer. His North Carolina teams win because he inspires his players to be competitive, to be aggressive, to settle for nothing less than victory.

On the wall in his office he has hung this sign: People Don't Care How Much You Know Until They Know How Much You Care. "That is the critical element in coaching women," Dorrance says. "You can't get me to do anything unless you care about me first. Soccer is not that important to them. Connection is."[1]

In his book *The Vision of a Champion*, Dorrance writes that being passive, or giving in so no one will be offended, is "the way our culture tells girls they have to gain respect. In the long run, though, you will gain people's respect, and in a way you'd rather have it, if you go after them on the soccer field."[2] Mia Hamm, one of his many star players, totally agrees. "I grew up always good at sports, but being a girl, I was never allowed to feel as good about it as the guys were," she says. "My toughness wasn't celebrated. But then I came here, and it was okay to want to be the best. I loved that I didn't have to apologize for the fact that I got upset for missing a goal."

Four-time All American Cindy Parlow explains, "Girls don't like to compete. We want to be friends. It's hard to create that atmosphere where conflict and competition are okay. That's what Anson has created for us."[3]

Even before the season starts, he holds weekly meetings with his players to psych them up on the playing field. One key area he addresses is leadership. A common problem in women's sports stems from being told from a very early age not to criticize each other. "Women ball things up inside a lot of times. We don't want to tell someone if they aren't doing a good job," Cat Reddick Whitehill points out. "We let it fester and bitterness tends to rise up, but what Anson has done is he's made this [an] atmosphere where you can't let it ball up. You have these meetings with each other. You have individual meetings with Anson where he tells you right away where you stand in the program and his expectations for you."

Dorrance feels that too much yelling at women players is not productive. After watching the way legendary North Carolina basketball coach Dean Smith ran his practices, Dorrance decided to use a different method to instill high standards. He calls it the Competitive Cauldron (as discussed on p. 139). Every single time a player touches a soccer ball in practice, she is graded in some way. His charts include all sorts of drills, such as: Serving and Receiving, Figure-8 Dribbling, and Brazilian Technical Passing. From those evaluations he builds a report card. He regularly posts the rankings on a bulletin board for everyone to see. Because the system is so open, a player must accept responsibility for her own performance. As Tim Crothers wrote in his book *The Man Watching*, "Dorrance believes one of the primary advantages of the stats comes in their shock value. Invariably they expose an established player who isn't performing up to her capability or a talented freshman who isn't psychologically prepared for the competitive cauldron."[4]

"He has everything accounted for," says Cat Reddick Whitehill. "Any player looking at the chart is forced to think, 'I can't hide behind the stats here, because I'm not doing a good enough job.' There's no room for excuses."

Ali Hawkins agrees. "You can get upset to a certain extent about your playing time, but ultimately it's pretty reflective of how you rank on the team. I think that's part of it; he makes it as objective as soccer can be."

A player starts gaining Dorrance's respect in his Competitive Cauldron practices. Hawkins says that the stress of the practice would start high "and keep increasing until it got to a point where you thought you were going to crack. I think on the surface they did it so that when you got to a national championship game, that wasn't stressful. My practices were way more stressful than any game I ever played. I would get way more nervous for a hard, hard practice day than I would for a national championship game." In fact, one of Dorrance's most famous quotes, made while introducing Mia Hamm to the National Soccer Hall of Fame,

(continued on next page)

is, "The vision of a champion is someone who is bent over, drenched in sweat, at the point of exhaustion, when no one else is watching."

Above all, Dorrance believes that women players have to learn how to be aggressive. In *Vision of a Champion*, he gives an example of one way he judges a player's character. "One of the crucial aspects when we play with defensive presence is getting 'stuck in,' a common British expression for an aggressive player who gets in tackles, or sticks her face in where the ball is going, risking taking a knock or getting whacked," he writes. "We describe those without this all-out physical courage as hummingbirds. They sort of just go humming around the action."[5]

Yet even with this intense competitive environment, his players still feel valued as individuals and contributors. Whitehill notes that he doesn't rely just on charts to motivate his players to get better. "One of his greatest qualities is how good he is at communicating on a personal level. There's rarely a time where you don't know where you stand. If you ask, 'Anson, where do I stand?' he's going to tell you right away. I think that's a great quality in a coach and in a leader."

She also points out another intangible: picking players that fit well together. "If someone is an incredible soccer player but wouldn't fit in the team chemistry, then he's not going to recruit them." For him, "it is a family, and if you stick in a bad seed, then that can really ruin everything."

Dorrance's care about selecting the right players stems from his true concern for the team. Ali Hawkins talks about how his personal interest made her a better player. "I think that ultimately a lot of us end up looking at him almost as a father figure, because he cares so much. He really cares about your life. I would go into his office all the time. Ten percent of the time we would actually talk about soccer. Everything else would be covered — politics, religion, boyfriends, family, everything. I think that's why he's able to draw the best out of his players. They know that his priority is them as a person. They're willing to sacrifice that extra bit."

The closeness of his teams is cultivated in other ways as well. Here is what former Tar Heels All-American Lori Chalupny has to say: "The on-field experiences and winning a national championship and all that were so great. But I think some of my best experiences were off the field — the

Thanksgiving feast that we have every year, where Anson's brother shuts down his restaurant, and all the families and everybody get together. It's those little things that make it so special. It's not just a program, it's not just about soccer; it's really a family, and I'll feel a part of that family forever."[6]

The coach focuses on making every player, even those that aren't starting, feel included. Whitehill says, "Some of the girls that don't go to UNC [tell me], 'Man, you can be so annoying sometimes, because you just have this special bond amongst y'all. I get sick and tired of hearing about the Tar Heels.'" She smiles. "We don't mean to do that, we don't want to annoy anybody, but it's just there, and other people that are outside the program can feel it, too."

The bonds that Dorrance forges with his players extend far beyond their playing days at UNC. "Anson really does value [a player] more as a person than as a soccer commodity," Ali Hawkins says. "I talk to players at other programs, and they always felt as though they were at their program for a set number of years and it was a soccer shop. After they left, their coach really couldn't care less about what they did or how they were doing. Anson is the exact opposite. He cares very little about our four years at Carolina in comparison to the arc of our lives."

As previously discussed, Dorrance's personal attention to his players is shown especially in his practice of writing senior letters, which comment on each student's athletic contribution and her core character. Whitehill recalls, "One of my favorite soccer moments is how he writes a letter to every senior. At the end of the season, he'll kick all the seniors out of the locker room, and he'll talk to all the underclassmen. He tells them, 'We play for our seniors, and you don't want to be the class that sends the senior class out with a loss.'"

Dorrance says, "Oftentimes the senior letter has more value to a girl that hasn't played much. I guess a lot of ways a player measures herself and certainly measures the affection a coach has for her is based on playing time. That's such a poor measure of a person's value. I'm not one of these people that really feels that athletic ability has a long-term redeeming value, unless it is in the context of where you've learned something from your sport that will allow you to contribute your humanity." He especially feels this way about his reserve players. "I

(continued on next page)

think [they] get the sense that, 'You know what, he does care about me. He has seen the things in me that have value.'" He doesn't overlook the contributions of players just because they've had limited playing time. "What I try to do in the senior letter is basically let them know that I've certainly been watching them, and I do have huge respect for who they are."

Dorrance's approach certainly resonated with Ali Hawkins. She recalls, "I remember I was walking with ten other girls. The coaches had just gotten back from a graduate's wedding. I asked, 'Would you guys invite the coaches to your wedding?' Every single person there said they would invite Anson to their wedding. I thought that was pretty incredible."

DICK GOULD: Pressure Points

Dick Gould realized that too much stress on winning all season long could be counterproductive. Instead, he would start off in a lower key, then keep increasing the pressure as the season kept building. "I think it goes back to when I first started. I was so focused on, 'We have to do this. We have to do this. We have to get there.'" That first NCAA championship took a lot of weight off his shoulders. "Once we got there in 1973, that took so much pressure off of me in my own mind that I could look back, reflect, and say [to myself], 'Wait a minute. This was hard to do, because you were making it so hard to do.'"

Instead, he adopted a new approach. "I guess after that first championship I learned not to get too excited about any one victory or any one loss, just to keep everything positive and everything building. Then, as your competition gets a little bit nearer, you can start talking a little more about getting ready for the nationals. You don't do that at the first part of the season. You talk about that as you get nearer the nationals."

Alex O'Brien enjoyed that approach. "He always kept it fun and fresh. At the beginning of the year, I remember playing in an individual tournament that he didn't really care too much about. His focus was winning the NCAA Tournament. I was down in the first set, and he came up behind the fence and said, 'How's it going out there?' I said, 'Not too good, Coach.' He said, 'Hey, you got him right where you want him.' He turned around and walked off, and I'm thinking this guy's on another planet. What is he talking about? I got him right where I want him? I lost the match, but I'll never forget that. He taught me not to take myself too seriously."

Gould points out, "At Stanford, you really could use your initiative. No one was looking over your shoulder in a sport like mine where you don't have to win, go to a bowl game. I never felt any pressure. If I did, it was pressure I put on myself."

In a sport filled with high-strung athletes, that was the formula for one of the best coaching records of all time.

DICK GOULD

DAN GABLE: Learning from Defeat

An athlete leading a team by his example is well known in sports folklore. A coach leading by example is not. Retired Iowa wrestling coach Dan Gable (with Mike Uker in photo at left), however, took a hands-on approach to teaching his championship teams. He was that rare combination: an exceptional athlete who was also an outstanding coach.

The numbers speak for themselves. As a wrestler, Gable compiled an unbelievable record of 182–1 during his prep and college careers. He was undefeated in 64 prep matches, and was 118–1 at Iowa State. His only defeat came in the NCAA finals his senior year. After college, Gable added titles at the 1971 Pan American Games and the 1971 World Championships. In 1972, in Munich, Germany, he won a gold medal at the Summer Olympics without surrendering a single point to any of his opponents.

He went on to become the University of Iowa's all-time winningest wrestling coach. From 1977 to 1997, Gable's teams compiled a career record of 355–21–5. He coached 152 All-Americans, 45 national champions, 106 Big Ten champions, and 12 Olympians, including four gold, one silver, and three bronze medalists. As part of his winning percentage of .932, the Hawkeyes won 21 consecutive Big Ten championships and nine consecutive (1978–86) NCAA Championships. He was a three-time Olympic head coach (1980, 1984, and 2000), and the 1984 Olympic team, which featured four Hawkeyes, won seven gold medals.[7] When ESPN compiled its 20th-century list of notable sports figures, Dan Gable was chosen as one of the top coaches of all time.

He started off in the more traditional role of an athlete leading others by his example. "As a high school sophomore, my head coach gave me the keys to the gym," he says. He tried to convince his teammates to come work out with him at six-thirty in the morning. "No one really came at first. Pretty soon most of them joined me. I think this was when I started wanting to become a coach. From an early age, my friends saw that I was helping them to become a better wrestler — and maybe that helped me get into coaching."

As dejected as he was after his one loss — the devastating end to his college career — Dan did not stop looking out for others. He remembers that another member of his team was so upset by Dan's loss that he didn't want to fight his own match. "He was three or four weights after me. I was recovering from [my] loss, sitting in the locker room, and the shower was on. I was kind of hiding out because people were hugging me and patting me on the back. I looked in the shower, and it was the guy that was supposed to be on deck. I asked him what the heck he was doing, and he said, 'Gable, I've never wrestled in the lineup when you've lost, and I'm not about to now.'" That really shook Dan up. "It took my mind off the loss and put my mind right into coaching. I looked at him and said, 'If you don't wrestle this match, it's going to hurt me more.' So he thought about it, and it took about two seconds for him to get his clothes on and get out there and win that match."

Gable transferred what he had learned on the mats to the coaching profession. After serving as an assistant coach at Iowa for four years, he took over the head coaching job. Yet, he didn't stop wrestling, as many of his students remember very well.

Bruce Kinseth won an NCAA championship for the Hawkeyes in 1979. He finished his collegiate career by pinning his way through the Big Ten and NCAA tournament. He was also named the Outstanding Wrestler at the national championship. He says he and his coach were the same weight class. "I was a 150-pounder, and he won the Olympics at 149 and a half." Gable had no problem getting down on the mat with his students. "At the end of practice every day it would be 5:30," Kinseth recalls, "and no one would be in the room but Gable and me. We wrestled a tremendous amount, and that's really what made a difference to me. I just kept getting beat on and beat on. You know, you don't make the same mistake twice. I'm a slow learner, but I continued to learn and get better and pick up a lot. That really made a big difference for me."

Nor did the coach only take on people his size. He would wrestle every kid on the team, showing them all of the techniques they would need to compete at the highest level. Jim Zabel, an Iowa broadcaster, remarked to ESPN, "I asked Lou Banach, when he was the NCAA championship heavyweight, 'What's the toughest thing you ever went through?' He said, 'Getting up at six o'clock in the morning and wrestling Gable. He could whip me, and I was a heavyweight.'"[8]

(continued on next page)

Gable didn't allow his students to slack off. Chad Zaputil, part of Gable's championship teams in the early 1990s, recalls, "He was an excellent motivator. It didn't matter what kind of kid it was, either. You could just see he could take a mix-and matched group of all kinds of athletes and get them motivated." He adds, "You didn't want to disappoint Gable. You wanted to train the hardest."

His grueling practices became legendary. As a wrestler himself, Gable had learned one lesson very well: "Gold medals aren't really made of gold. They're made of sweat, determination, and a hard-to-find alloy called guts." One of his former wrestlers, Royce Alger, jokes about how tough the practices were. "Every workout was about trying to find out how much more tired he could get his athletes. In order to break people, there has to be some degree of physical torture." He laughs. "I would rather do 'time' than go back and do some of that stuff."[9]

"He had what he called 'buddy carries,'" says his biographer, Nolan Zavoral. "There are 80 steps from the floor of the Hawkeye Arena to the balcony. You would put someone else your weight on your back and run up those steps with him."[10]

Yet Gable knew that all that training would pay off during the match. He didn't just want his athletes to be their strongest when their opponent was starting to wear down. He wanted them to succeed because they had the courage to give it their all during the tough practices. He once said, "The first period is won by the best technician. The second period is won by the kid in the best shape. The third period is won by the kid with the biggest heart."

Chad Zaputil remembers a telling detail. "If somebody said they were going to do something and they didn't follow through, he would give them a slip of paper, and on it was the word 'dependability,'" he says. That meant "fulfilling what you consented to do even when it means unexpected sacrifices."

Though all athletes shared the same grueling practices, Gable treated each one as an individual. "I came to realize that wrestlers came in all shapes, sizes, and backgrounds," he says. "I had bullies wrestle for me, and I also had rich kids wrestle for me." Bruce Kinseth remembers how that approach worked for him. "He was very good at coaching different kinds of wrestlers and athletes. Like me; I wasn't that talented. I had to work really hard. I was kind of like putty that he had to turn into chiseled steel."

Chad Zaputil said Gable's style of motivation "was entirely different for everybody." Any team has a wide range of personalities. Knowing what makes each one of them tick is crucial in a wrestling program. "Some kids are more intellectual. Some kids are there from when the sun comes up to when it goes down for their work ethic," Zaputil says. "What [Gable] did so well was to know how to help each kid reach his goals."

Equally as important, he made everyone feel like a part of the team. One of his assistant coaches, Mark Johnson, notes, "Every team rule was set to the individual. He knew everybody so well: what made them tick, what was wrong with their girlfriend, did they go out the night before."[11]

Zaputil relished the close attention. "He was a coach that really did care about his athletes. I'm sure there are successful coaches that run their program like a business or a factory, and I never really felt like it was like that at Iowa. I felt like it was more of a family." Bruce Kinseth agrees about the team camaraderie. "Certainly in my era there was a tremendous closeness between the whole wrestling community, and it started with Gable."

Dan Gable succeeded in part because he never allowed all that winning to go to his head. "I'm the kind of guy that gets over quickly what I've accomplished," he remarks. He believes that you have to guard against success because it will set you up for a fall. He had that incredible streak as a wrestler himself, only to lose in his very last match in college. "It doesn't go away, that type of loss, and you analyze it. Now it's 41 years later, and I'm still analyzing it." He suffered the same fate at the end of his Iowa team's streak of nine national championships in a row. "I put myself in a position to be the only coach in D-1 history that would have won ten straight national championships at the time, back in 1987, and wouldn't you know, I lost that one, too," he says. "We were pretty heavily favored to win it." For Gable, the only cure for losing was to work harder.

Athletes coming into the Iowa program knew what was in store before they ever set foot on campus. "Everybody knew Dan Gable coming in. He was a legend already and an Olympic champion," Bruce Kinseth says. "I knew about it. I read a book someone had written about his work ethic." Gable was the guy who was quoted saying, "Right out of high school I never had the fear of getting beat, which is how most people lose." All of the practices and matches taught his players to rise to their challenges. "I was one of those guys that was a product of that environment," Kinseth adds. "Because I came in and did everything that was asked, you couldn't help but succeed at some level.

"First coming in, you were a little in awe of Dan Gable. Everybody grew

(continued on next page)

up hearing stories of Dan Gable," he says. Yet the coach was a humble person. He would "sit down, talk with you, talk with everybody that comes through the program. It's just the kind of person he is." That started from the very beginning. "He made you feel like a part of the program, even though you might have only been on campus for a day. It didn't matter how long you had been around. It was not a business to him. It was his life. He lived and breathed the sport."

Dan Gable firmly believed that "once you've wrestled, everything else in life is easy." That's because the one-on-one nature of the sport so often determines who will be the winner. "More enduringly than any other sport," he says, "wrestling teaches self-control and pride. Some have wrestled without great skill — none has wrestled without pride."

Bruce Kinseth was a perfect example of this philosophy. "Coming out of high school from a small town in Iowa," he remarks, "I wasn't sure I had what it took to succeed in wrestling. I was around all these guys that were two- and three-time state champs. They all had a lot of confidence." Going through the tough day-in and day-out training at Iowa made all the difference. He became a believer in one of Gable's favorite sayings: "If there is an opportunity in front of you, take it." Kinseth might have started out without much confidence, but he made himself into a champion. "Frankly, coming in on day one, I didn't know if I would be able to keep up with the workouts. Then I became the leader."

"A lot of us still keep in touch. I talk to teammates, and I think a lot of them still keep in touch with Gable for that reason. He's a big part of our lives because we poured blood, sweat, and tears into the program," Zaputil says. "There's nobody that has done more than him. He expected a lot out of his athletes and he put a lot of effort into it."

Kinseth agrees. "My best friends today are the guys I roomed with at Iowa and wrestled with. We travel on vacation together. We go to all these places together and do everything together. I don't know if all the wrestling groups were like that."

Gable thinks that the lessons he teaches about wrestling will carry on throughout a student's life. He wants to know "how my athletes that I coached are doing today. If I do a great job, then the people [I coached] will do a better job." He cites one example at Boise State, whose wrestling team has become a powerhouse. "Their wrestling coach [Greg Randall] was one of my favorite athletes, and I coached him." He is proud when "you've made an impact, and it doesn't stop making an impact."

What he learned from defeat also contributed to the longer-lasting lessons he taught his athletes. It's a part of sports and a part of life. Chad Zaputil finished second three years in a row in the national championship, and yet his coach stayed right with him. Gable once famously said, "Pain is nothing compared to what it feels like to quit. Give everything you got today, for tomorrow may never come." No matter what student came into his program, he taught that same never-say-die philosophy. "In any defeat, you have to learn from it and get better tomorrow," Zaputil says. "I think that's the beauty of the way he was. Everybody gets beat at some point, even Dan Gable. How you react to that is a measure of what type of person you are. If he ever suffered a defeat, he came back ten times stronger. He's a unique individual. When you lose, you don't want that to make you weaker, you want that to make you stronger."

Bruce Kinseth agrees that what he learned as a wrestler has carried over into his adult life, working in the hotel business. "I had a hard work ethic coming in. So I came out a better person, a better businessman, a tougher businessman. Today, if somebody gets in my face, which happens more than you think, whether it's lenders or buyers or competitors, sometimes you just have to tell people to shove it. If you get in there and scrap with them, they back down."

A pep talk goes only so far in motivating athletes. To produce champions year in and year out, Dan Gable went much farther. He used his body, and his heart, to teach every single kid in his program. The results have gone down in history.

Chapter 6

FINDING YOUR X-FACTOR

"WE WILL DISCOVER THE NATURE OF OUR PARTICULAR GENIUS WHEN WE STOP TRYING TO CONFORM TO OUR OWN OR TO OTHER PEOPLE'S MODELS, LEARN TO BE OURSELVES, AND ALLOW OUR NATURAL CHANNEL TO OPEN."
— SHAKTI GAWAIN

Each previous chapter highlighted an aspect of coaching that a number of championship coaches have incorporated into their approach. Care about your team members. Communicate directly and meaningfully. Keep it simple. Motivate and inspire through empowerment and individualized tactics. Weave these common threads into your strategy for leading others to achievement. At the same time, these strategies alone are not enough.

What is the missing element? As the ancient saying goes, know thyself. Whether you are coaching on the sideline or in the boardroom, understand your strengths. Spend time and energy developing these talent areas. All of the championship coaches in this book possess a keen self-awareness, accompanied by a comfort level with who they are and a willingness to develop their talents.

Understand and value what you bring to the table. Build on your strengths. None of these championship coaches is perfect; they are humans with flaws. But they honed the facets of their character that helped create championship environments. When you can be yourself and you strive to be the best version of yourself, you encourage others to be themselves. And in an environment where people are genuine, good things happen.

The coaches within these pages know who they are. They're authentic. They are true to themselves. They don't apologize for it, and they don't boast about it. They have confidence, tempered by humility, and a sense of conviction, essential qualities for a leader.

They have been shaped by the people who raised them, inspired by the mentors they've admired, and toughened through experiences along the journey. We are all products of our environment to a certain degree. During interviews with these incredible coaches, it was fascinating to learn their secrets to developing a championship mentality — the x-factors that set them apart.

In 2001, the Gallup organization unveiled an assessment called the Clifton StrengthsFinder (now 2.0 version) in the book *Now, Discover Your Strengths*. The StrengthsFinder is based on over 40 years of research on what helps people at the top of their fields achieve success in careers such as athletics, education, business, medicine, and politics. Donald Clifton wondered what would happen if we studied "What is right with people?" instead of focusing so much on what needs to be fixed. Through the course of his research, 34 primary themes emerged. And the common finding among the top achievers was this: they each thoroughly understood their own talents and made a concerted effort to develop those talents into strengths that they utilized along their path to success.

Think for a moment about what your unique strengths are. What sets you apart from your colleagues and peers? What do the members of your team need from you to function at their optimal level? This is important information.

You may want to complete the StrengthsFinder assessment to clarify and validate your strengths. And when you get the results, reflect on how you can continue to build up and make the most of these strengths to create a championship environment for those around you. The better you know yourself, the more efficient you will be at utilizing your unique talents and strengths to the utmost potential.

During the process of understanding your championship qualities, tame self-deprecation and keep your ego in check. Strive for a balance between honoring your strengths and understanding your weaknesses. Be honest with yourself and authentic with others. When you truly know yourself, you know the good, the bad, and the ugly. A clear picture of your faults keeps you humble. When you are aware of the areas you struggle with, you can surround yourself with others who make up for the traits you lack. Knowing your strengths helps you shine.

And here's another benefit that stems from being truly comfortable with who you are: you are secure enough to encourage other people to let their lights shine, too.

Perhaps the following poem sums it up best. John Wooden first read it early in his teaching and coaching career in the 1930s. The meaning of the message resonated with Wooden for the rest of his life.

As he sat in the den of his Encino, California, condominium in 2004, he closed his eyes and recited the poem for me:

> *"No written word,*
>
> *Nor spoken plea*
>
> *Can teach our youth what they should be.*
>
> *Nor all the books on all the shelves.*
>
> *It's what the teachers are themselves."*
>
> — Anonymous

CHALK TALK:

- ☒ **UNDERSTAND AND DEVELOP YOUR STRENGTHS. BE TRUE TO WHO YOU ARE.**

- ◯ **SEEK OUT MENTORS WITH SIMILAR STRENGTHS WHO HAVE ACHIEVED SUCCESS.**

- ☒ **ENCOURAGE YOUR TEAM MEMBERS TO IDENTIFY AND HONE THEIR STRENGTHS. GIVE THEM ROOM TO SHINE.**

PROFILES

TONY DUNGY: Paying It Forward

Tony Dungy won a Super Bowl as a player — Pittsburgh Steelers in 1978 — and as a head coach — Indianapolis Colts in 2007. He retired from coaching in 2009 and is now a studio analyst for NBC's NFL coverage. He has also authored three best-selling books with coauthor Nathan Whitaker: *Quiet Strength*, *Uncommon*, and *The Mentor Leader*. His most recent book with Whitaker is *The One Year Uncommon Life Daily Challenge*. Dungy believes that two of the keys to his success as a coach were being true to himself and creating an environment in which members of his team felt encouraged and free to be the best version of themselves.

"When [former Steelers head coach who won four Super Bowls] Coach [Chuck] Noll talked to me about going into coaching, that was probably the greatest thing that happened to me, because I did end up working my first eight years in [Pittsburgh] for a great example, for a guy who did it the right way and who understood how to reach people. As I started working for him, then I had to think about developing my personality, because that was the one piece of advice he gave me. He said, 'Number one, you have to be yourself. Don't try to copy me or anybody else. Use your assets and God-given gifts.' My first few years, I asked myself, 'What type of coach am I going to become?' I always thought back to the coaches that I had been around, guys that I would like to have played for and then the coaches who coached me. Who helped me the most? To me, it was the encouraging people who built you up and helped you become a better player. That was Coach Noll's thing all the time. Your only job is to help your players play better. It's not to be a disciplinarian. It's not to have all the answers. Don't think of yourself in any other way, but how can you help your players play the best they can play? With that in mind, I kind of formed the way I wanted to coach."

Dungy is big on mentoring. This makes a lot of sense, considering the enormous role his mentors played during the course of his journey to a Super Bowl victory. Dungy developed a solid sense of who he was as a person and who he wanted to be as a coach. He has been very open about

(continued on next page)

the fact that he is a Christian and uses Christian principles as a coach. He sought out mentors who aligned with this approach and who'd been successful. Take a lesson from Dungy. Seek out people you admire who share your coaching or management style. Look for people who exhibit the talents you possess — people who have attained success by developing these strengths and being true to themselves. Having solid mentors is especially helpful when you need some extra encouragement that your style and strengths can lead to success. Dungy needed this kind of support at times, and now he's paying it forward by mentoring young coaches.

"I was climbing up the ladder and doing well and having success, but then you get people telling you, 'Well, to get to the next level when you're a coordinator or a head coach, you can't do it that way. You have to do this, this, and this from the world's perspective.' But seeing guys like Coach [Tom] Osborne and [former Washington Redskins head coach who won three Super Bowls] Joe Gibbs and [former Dallas Cowboys head coach who won two Super Bowls] Tom Landry have that type of success and looking at John Wooden, all of them were real, real inspirational for me because sometimes you do think, 'Well, maybe this [approach] just works in high school, or maybe it just works in college, or maybe it works when you're a position coach, maybe people are right.' But I just kept seeing guys have that success and not deviate from their path of honoring the Lord, and that was inspiring to me. My last few years, that was the motivation for me to stay involved with it, to think maybe there were some other young coaches out there that needed that same type of role model, to see that you can stick to your guns and do it your way and be successful no matter what sport or what level.

"I really considered leaving probably five to eight years before I did, but I wanted to show that you could coach with Christian principles and still be successful. I wanted to show other guys that you could do that. I did have my principles in place, and that was another thing I would say early on to the guys [on the team]. 'As a Christian, this is how I'm going to coach you. I don't expect everybody to buy into my philosophy of life, but I'm going to coach you this way. I'm going to treat you with respect. I'm not going to curse at you or use profanity. I'm not going to yell at you or try to embarrass you on the field or in public. If you need that to be successful, then come visit me after this meeting, and we'll try to trade you to another team where you can get people to yell at you and curse at you.'

"I never had anybody come up to me and say, 'Coach, I really need that. Would you mind trading me, because I don't think I can function in this environment?' But it was important to me to let guys know what my life was all about. That way, if we ever had a need to converse, they could feel free. I'm certainly going to try to steer you in the direction that I want you to go, but I'm not going to be demanding that you do it my way. It was important to me to be myself. I am a Christian coach. That was a big part of my motivation, especially the second half of my coaching career."

Dungy was aware of his values and his strengths, and he stayed true to himself. Because of that, he was able to create an atmosphere of mutual respect on his NFL teams. He treated men like men and meted out discipline with a gentle but firm hand. This approach was extraordinarily effective — team members worked extra hard in order to maintain the empowering environment they so enjoyed. He also helped them understand that the best chance of team success was through individual effort. He encouraged each person to be the best version of himself.

"You want to create that environment where it's not just you demanding it and the players doing it because they're afraid of you, but for them to realize that this is the best way. This is how they can function well. Once they get that feeling, they want to keep it going. They want to have ownership of it. That's what you're really trying to create.

"We talked about winning; obviously that was what we wanted to do, but I always said to the team, 'We are going to make this an environment that you enjoy while you're winning.' I believe you can do that, and that's what I wanted to do. We wanted to make it so that guys didn't want to leave. Then, it became the veteran players helping and saying, 'Hey, don't mess this up. We have a coach that respects us and understands us. Let's win so we can keep this.' The players wanted new members on the team who bought into the idea of winning and enjoying the environment that had been created.

"I felt I probably didn't get some [head coaching] jobs because when people asked me, 'How are you going to discipline? How are you going to motivate?' I described building it this way, and they didn't think I could

(continued on next page)

get that done. 'Well, you won't win,' they'd say. They didn't believe in the model, but I felt like if we could win, make it an enjoyable experience, and have that mutual respect, then the players could come to me when they had suggestions with ways that we could do things better and know that their voice would be heard and that family issues would always come first over football. With those kinds of things, I think you build a mutual respect that causes that unity. I talked a lot about their reputation and how people looked at them. 'Hey, there's just 53 guys on the team, and we have 51 of you doing great things and two people kind of messing up the apple cart. Then everyone refers to that. Everyone's saying that you're all tied together, so the two reflect on all the others. We don't want that. We don't want two guys defining our whole team, so you guys are going to police it a little bit and make sure we have the right kind of guys here.'

"At the very first team meeting, I'd say, 'Hey, here's what we're going to be like, and you may think that what you do individually doesn't reflect on everybody else and as long as you're doing your job and winning, that's all that counts. No, it doesn't, and here's why.' That's something that I learned from Art Rooney, Sr., the owner of the Pittsburgh Steelers when we first got there. When I was a rookie in 1977, he told the rookie class, 'From now on, wherever you go, you are going to reflect on the Steelers organization, the city of Pittsburgh, and the National Football League. You are not just Tony Dungy walking out in the street. You are now Tony Dungy the Steeler, Tony Dungy the NFL player, and you are going to represent Pittsburgh, the Steelers, and the NFL.' It took me a little while to grasp that, but I saw that he was right, and that's what I always wanted to point out to my guys on day one. Off the field, we're going to reflect that. On the field, it's how we do things together. If we are unified, we are going to have a much better chance of success."

When discipline was in order, Dungy was respectful yet firm. "I would always start it individually, get the facts, talk to the player, and make my decision in terms of what I wanted to do and how I wanted to discipline. But then I would talk to the team about it as a whole. 'Hey, here's what happened. Here's what we decided to do and here's why. Now, this is our teammate. We're going to stand by him, but here are the ramifications of it.' If we ever got someone for whom the discipline didn't seem to work, that's when we had to make decisions. Fortunately, we didn't have too many of those guys. We had a couple of guys early on, when I started in Tampa [as head coach of the Tampa Bay Buccaneers]. That's when we'd say, 'This guy's not a part of our team anymore because he didn't seem to respond to the way we want to do things.' Once guys got the message that this was important to you, it became a line that not many of them wanted to cross, because they wanted to stay there. It was fairly easy. It wasn't anything that ever became an issue, because guys said, 'There are certain things that I can't do because Coach doesn't accept it,' and it goes with the territory of being a Colt or being a Buccaneer."

Dungy stayed true to himself. His success was bred from a strong desire to help others fully develop their potential, combined with the courage and persistence to implement his faith-based values in a coaching world where that wasn't always popular. He understood what he was all about, and he sought mentors along the way who inspired him and reinforced his choices.

Look back on the people and events that have shaped you into who you are today. Who are the top five most influential people in your life? What qualities do they possess that you admire? How have they helped you grow as a person? Take some time to reflect on these questions. Knowing where you come from helps you understand where you are going. Again, self-awareness is crucial. The more you know yourself, the better you can apply your strengths, and the more effective you'll be in encouraging others to let their strengths shine.

LOU HOLTZ: Learning from His Uncle Lou

 Lou Holtz, who led college football teams for 33 seasons, now lends his insight and entertains college football fans on ESPN each fall during the season. He possesses a distinct brilliance of communicating and connecting with people through humor and inspiring others to achieve their best. His legendary style and personal values were formed in large part thanks to his relationship with his beloved Uncle Lou. Humor, dependability, and a willingness to sacrifice were Uncle Lou's legacy to Coach Holtz. From sleeping on the couch so little Lou and his family had a place to stay, to joining the military, to attending all but one of Holtz's Notre Dame games, Uncle Lou enthusiastically answered the call to serve and to offer a supportive presence.

"My uncle Lou had the greatest impact on my life other than my wife (Beth, whom Holtz has been married to for 50 years]. At the start of World War II, we were in Follansbee [West Virginia]. I was going into the third grade. It was the Depression. There was one bedroom for the whole family, a kitchen, and a half-bath, and that was it. When the war began, my dad went in to the Navy, so we moved to East Liverpool, Ohio, to live with my mother's parents during the war. Uncle Lou was a junior in high school there. I don't remember what time of the year we moved there, but I met him then. There were only two bedrooms in the home. It was a rather nice home compared to the one we came from, but they moved Uncle Lou into the living room, where he slept. My mother, sister, and I used the one bedroom, and my grandparents used the other bedroom. We had one bath. Uncle Lou was a football player, and that was big in East Liverpool. We'd go to the games, and we'd watch him play. He was good. Then, sometimes at night, he would take me down on the corner with the big guys to stand there. He'd take me to a movie on occasion, and he'd talk to me all the time. I'll never forget one time he told me, 'Next time Grandpa says something, tell him that's propaganda.' I said, 'What?' He said, 'Oh, it's funny.' Well, I said it to Grandpa, and he whacked me. I said to Uncle Lou, 'You said it would be funny.' He said, 'I said I would find it funny.'

"Every night after football he would fight with Grandpa, trying to get him to sign the papers to let him to join the military, because he wasn't 18 yet. It was a big argument. Finally, he did, so Uncle Lou went into the Navy. He was there about four months, and the war ended. He gets out, and they had a 52–20 club, which meant that if you applied for jobs for 52 weeks, you got 20 dollars. Well, Uncle Lou was single. He didn't want to work, so he would go apply for jobs he wasn't going to get. My grandpa got mad because that wasn't the way you lived in this country. My grandma and grandpa were both immigrants. They weren't born here. They threw him out of the house, so he came and lived with us.

"I tell you, he was just funny, clever, loved football," Holtz continues, his admiration of his uncle very clear. When Holtz's school started a football team, Uncle Lou became the coach. "I'm in the fifth grade, and I was really small, but I played with the eighth graders because he was the coach and he was my friend. So now, I'm in high school, and he's working as a sales clerk at Montgomery Ward. We would meet every day at the American Pool Hall, play pool, and talk. Then, I went to college, and he married a beautiful girl. (They were married 40 years before he died. She's still living and still a beautiful person.) Then, he started a little Sears catalog store. That thing grew and grew, and he became a successful entrepreneur. He ended up having about 12 people work for him. Everybody loved him. He had a sense of humor. So now, I'm in college. Every time I came back from college, if I had a day, I saw Uncle Lou and his wife. I was dating two girls. They loved Beth and didn't really care for the other one. What they thought had a big influence on who I married. I married Beth, and we just celebrated our 50th wedding anniversary.

"Now, I'm in coaching. Every time I went back, they'd come to games. I go to Notre Dame. In my 11 years at Notre Dame, he missed one game — home or away, bowl game, etc. He died a few years after I left Notre Dame, but he was a great character. He was involved in the community, but here's a guy who went from the 52–20 club to being an entrepreneur to being very involved in athletics in the community. This would be typical Uncle Lou. He was on the board of the quarterback club. They'd meet in a restaurant. He would say, 'Everybody, let's throw in two dollars apiece for the tip.' There'd be ten people there. He'd take the 20 dollars and say to the waitress, 'Here's my tip. I don't know if they're going to tip you any.'

"That was typical of what he would do and his sense of humor. His character, his integrity, his values, and believing in just being a good person, and he certainly was."

Holtz incorporated humor and a joyful spirit into coaching as much as he could — appreciating each day and giving others a laugh even if it was at his own expense.

(continued on next page)

"I'm amazed at how many players can impersonate me. They all can impersonate my lisp. Also, we went by LLH [Louis Leo Holtz] time. When I talk, I think first of all, you have to have something you want to say and a burning desire to say it. Whatever I said, I believed in my heart at that time. Also, I always inject humor into what I say.

"Uncle Lou had the greatest sense of humor, funnier than all get-out. I think that helped me form my sense of humor. Even in my pep talks I always had a few jokes, because that's me. You have to have fun with what you're doing. Every day, I walked out on the practice field, the first thing I said was, 'Get a smile on your face and a song in your heart. Boy, am I glad to be here. What a great day to work. This is a great day. How lucky we are to be here. Do you know people pay money in the summer to come stay here? We get to stay here for free and get an education. Do you see how lucky you are? You have to be excited, because it could be snowing.' That's what I would say. I believed it. I'd walk around practice and say to the players, 'People pay me thousands of dollars to travel all over this world to speak, and I talk to you for free. You don't even take a damn note. You've got to be the dumbest people in this world.' Then, they'd just laugh."

Holtz's Uncle Lou provided a model for who he wanted to become as a person. Holtz valued the qualities that Uncle Lou stood for — humor, dependability, sacrifice — and he embraced them and encouraged his team members to embrace them during his coaching career. Additionally, Holtz developed a sense of how he could help others become the best they could be by utilizing a strategy he initially learned from his high school English teacher, Glenda Dunlop. According to Holtz, at 5'1", 100 lbs, she was no-nonsense and tough as nails. The expectation was clear: nothing less than your best effort.

"Not only did you have to know the proper grammar, you had to know the rule. I got the fifth-highest grade in her class, which was a C+. I'll tell you right now, I used to complain that the only thing that was good about it was there was a girl in class named Sandra Dick, whom I was madly in love with and she didn't know it. That's the only reason I went to that class. Ms. Dunlop was mean, nasty, refused to take anything less than your best effort. She was tough. And fortunately I had her.

"I never realized the impact Glenda Dunlop had on me until I went to college [at Kent State]. All of a sudden in college, you have to be able to write, and you have to be able to express yourself. Those two things are critical, and that's when it became clear to me that I was pretty well prepared at college in that one area, and it was just because of her."

Ms. Dunlop's tough standards were effective. This experience planted the seed for Holtz that setting high expectations for others helps them be the best they can be. And discipline goes hand in hand with expectations. You have to consistently steer your team onto the path you believe leads to success.

"You have to be tough," Holtz says. "It's like the two guys who got a puppy. You have one guy that loved the puppy and allowed it to do anything it wanted to do. Everybody thought how great that was. The other guy got a puppy, and the first thing he did was put a choke collar on it. Everybody said how mean and nasty he was. A year later, the guy takes the choke collar off the dog, and the dog runs around the neighborhood and everybody loves him and enjoys him. Why? The dog knew what it could do and what it couldn't do, the parameters. The guy who loved the puppy and allowed it to do whatever it wanted, he could never give it any freedom. Sometimes, you have to put a choke collar on people when they're younger, until they learn what to do and what not to do. I cared about the freshmen, but they were still freshmen. They came here to become us. We didn't bring them here to become them. You came here and joined us because you wanted to be us. It's simple."

Holtz further developed his strength of drawing the best out of others under the tutelage of Woody Hayes, the legendary Ohio State football coach. Hayes understood that helping individuals recognize and stretch their own strengths ultimately strengthens the team. Holtz was able to pursue his coaching career with the confidence that holding people to a high standard is an effective method for achieving success. In fact, he encouraged his team members to hold themselves to a higher standard than anyone else had for them. In this way he developed teams full of individuals who were striving to be the best version of themselves. And when everyone is working to that end, the team is going to rise to its optimal potential.

Holtz continues, "The main thing I learned from Woody Hayes, among other things, was that as a leader, a coach, and a parent, our obligation's not to be well liked, our obligation is not to be their friend. Our obligation in a leadership role is to make [the players] the best that they can be. Not everybody can be an All-American, not everybody can be All-Conference, and not everybody can be first team, but everybody *can* be the best that they're capable of being. Let's not settle for less. What I found is that most people don't understand how much talent and ability they have. Consequently,

(continued on next page)

they're willing to settle for a lower standard than they're capable of achieving. You're not cheating the team as much as you're cheating yourself when you fail to realize the true talent and ability that you have. Morale on a football team doesn't come when you're winning, but morale comes when the players are getting better. No matter what, if the players feel they're getting better, they're going to feel good about themselves and what they're doing. That's all I wanted, just to make sure that we got better at doing something every single day.

"Players sometimes rebel against coaches when, as a coach, you see what they're capable of and you [set] their standard much higher than they have for themselves. Because you see the potential they have, they think you're being unfair and trying to make them be great or putting unreasonable requirements or standards on them. If my standard is here, and the player has a higher standard than I have for him, then that's great. Always have a higher standard of expectation for yourself than anybody else does for you. Usually, when a player thought I was mistreating him or being tough on him, it was because my standards were higher than his. It shouldn't be that way. He thinks you're being unfair to him. You treat all players fairly, you do not treat them all equally. There's a difference.

"For example, let's say you have an individual who comes from a broken home, who didn't have a strong guiding influence on how to do things. My son Skip [now the head football coach at South Florida] played for me my first year [at Notre Dame]. He and three other players were late. After practice, the team gathered around and I said, 'You four out here. You were late.' I gave them up-and-downs and ran them until they were tired, and I said, 'Okay, you three are done. Skip, you aren't.' I ran Skip in front of that team until he almost died. Finally, the players started to gather in [so] I couldn't do it anymore. That's the only reason I quit. Skip came in the next day and said, 'I deserved to run like the others, but I didn't deserve to run more than them. You were unfair to me.' I said, 'No, I was fair to you. I was fair to them. I wasn't equal. I raised you. You knew better. They didn't know better. As my son, you knew all your life that being on time is important. They didn't know. They'll know next time.' And I reminded Skip that your standards and expectations should be always be higher than anybody else's for you."

Holtz also relied on his talent for observing people to learn as much as he could about effective coaching. He watched the coaches around him to see what worked and what didn't work. Sometimes, we get so caught up in what we're doing that we fail to notice the coaching styles of others. But that is a rich source of information, and if you pay attention to how others operate, you will glean valuable knowledge about how to attain success. A passion for learning combined with a talent for observing others helped Holtz refine his coaching strengths.

"Well, being a younger person than most of my peers and not being a particularly good athlete — partly because of ability and partly because of age — I was always the one that was making mistakes or wasn't as good as the others. I remember this one drill we had in football that I kept trying to do what the coach wanted, but he obviously felt that it wasn't what it should be. You play for different people. I'm one of these guys that looks at things and says, why is this person successful and why is this one not?

"When I was on a staff — and it was an excellent staff — we had two coaches that screamed and hollered a lot. Players loved one coach and resented the other. What was the difference? What I noticed was the one coach got on the players because he wanted them to be good. The other guy got on the players only when the media or other people were around. He wanted to show how superior he was and what a great coach he was when the players weren't doing it the way he wanted it. That's why one breeds success and the other breeds contempt. You look at it and you say, 'It's not whether you get on them or not, but if you want them to be good, then let's go right to performance to make sure we don't get on the performer.' It's just by studying people. Why is this person successful and why is he not? Why does this work? Why does this not work? That's all. I just looked at people and compared them. That's a thing I've done most of my life, and I still find I do it today. Why is this person good on TV and this one not as good?"

Holtz continues to develop his strengths in his career as a broadcaster, inserting humor, maintaining high standards for college teams around the country, and offering inspirational messages to bring out the best in others. And he is just as dependable and ever present for his former players as Uncle Lou was for him.

Holtz recounts "Well, what I said to them was, 'If you give me everything that you can for four years, I'll be there for 40 for you.' I think that's my obligation. They do the right thing for four years, and there's not a week that goes by that I don't hear from at least four or five players. Either they got a

(continued on next page)

promotion or they need help or something, but I will. I'll do everything I can to help them, even if it's saying, 'No, this isn't the right thing for you.' You try to be honest with them. I enjoy hearing from them, and I'm glad that they realized they can always call on me for help."

Holtz is well aware of his strengths and knows how to help others develop their strengths. Just as he was influenced by Uncle Lou, you have been influenced by people in your life. As discussed earlier, reflect on the people who have positively impacted you and helped you recognize and foster your talents. Take the time to let them know what a difference they've made in your life.

ANDREA HUDY: "Foxhole Material"

Andrea Hudy, strength and conditioning coach at the University of Kansas, may have nine national championship rings, but growing up she was the kid sister in a family of five children. She is quick to point out that she may not be the smartest or the strongest or the most disciplined person, but she is definitely tough. In fact, when several of her Kansas colleagues were casually discussing who from the athletic department they'd want in their "foxhole" if ever that situation arose, every single one of them agreed on Hudy. She is foxhole material. Her toughness was honed through competitions with her siblings.

She describes her childhood as "a mix between *Fear Factor* and *Jackass*," where competitions with her siblings included numerous races and feats testing strength. Losers would have to do everything from drinking a Coke (that her brother had seasoned with Tabasco sauce), to running up and down the family's stone driveway in bare feet, to walking on an overturned welcome mat, again in bare feet, which were punctured by the sharp rubber nubs, to the most dreaded lost bet of all — having to eat Grandma's poppyseed bread.

Those crazy childhood games contributed to Hudy's development as a national championship coach. Now in her 17th year of coaching, she is widely considered the premier strength and conditioning coach in college athletics. She has served in that capacity for nine national championship teams: at Connecticut, she won two men's basketball, five women's basketball, and one men's soccer national championship, and at Kansas, men's basketball in 2008.

The competition with her siblings taught Hudy to rise to a challenge and be tough in the face of obstacles. And that toughness is evident today in her relentless effort to rise to the top when there is a competition. She is always up for a challenge. She recounts how she often joins the KU men's basketball coaches in jogging home after practice, but one morning she couldn't accompany them right away because she was wrapping up some things at work. "I asked Barry [Hinson] and Coach [Bill Self] if they were going on 23rd Street and Barry said, 'Yes, but you'll never catch us.' I said, 'What? What do you mean I'll never catch you? Now I *have* to catch you.'" And true to form, even with a 20-minute delayed start, Hudy caught them while they were still making their way home.

(continued on next page)

She would never ask a student-athlete to do something she wouldn't do herself. She has a gift for being able to determine what someone's potential is beyond what they even think they're capable of doing. And for those athletes who trust her, they are successful because they push past the limits they think exist to reach the goals she sets for them. Much like Coach Wooden, Hudy is able to bring out the best in people by demanding their highest effort.

Another quality that contributes to Hudy's success is her willingness and determination to choose the more difficult path. She never cuts a corner. Even dating back to her high school athletics days on the volleyball and basketball courts, she always cleared the corners as expected and always touched the line. "My world is black and white. You either do it or you don't. You either get it or you don't. The ball goes in the basket or it doesn't. You get a stop or you don't." These clear expectations are communicated directly to her student-athletes, and if they buy in, they choose the more difficult path just like Hudy does.

Speaking of difficult paths, Hudy has repeatedly had to prove herself in a man's world. She says, "It's not like I walk into a situation where a guy could get instant street credibility because he's a guy and he's big and he's bald. Every situation where I've been hired, I'm not their first choice. My belief is, 'Okay, give me a chance, and I'll show you what I can do and how we can do it.' I just hired a guy today. He's hired on stipulations; he has to meet standards. And you know what? I don't have any sympathy for that dude, because in every job I've ever taken the belief was, 'She can't do this.' I'm always behind the eightball. The question I get asked the most is how the guys take to you, and I think it goes back to the idea that everything is black or white. It's either you do something or you don't. There's no in-between. It just gets done.

"That's where the standard is set, with the very first workout. The baseball players came in and had the attitude, 'This is our weight room, and we're going to get our workout in.' I said, 'No, you aren't.' A couple of the freshmen thought, 'Who's this woman telling us how we're going to do it?' It took them an hour to get out of the locker room, which is by the weight room, because [they were so tired] they couldn't walk."

Hudy is tough. She demands the best others can give. And because she chooses the more difficult path, others have no opportunity to make excuses, no room to complain. It's a formula for greatness.

TOM OSBORNE: Living the Goal

Zach Wiegert, a three-year starter and All-American offensive lineman on the University of Nebraska's first national championship team, said that Tom Osborne always held true to his word. This led to building a culture of trust and team unity that motivated players and helped Osborne achieve sustained success, Wiegert believes.

"When he said something, he always meant it," says Wiegert, who won the Outland Trophy as the top interior lineman in the nation as a senior in 1994. "[Osborne] always backed it up. If we ran at the end of practice, he ran with us. He would say you need to eat healthier. Well, he always ate healthy. He'd tell us you don't need to be swearing at practice. Well, he doesn't swear. It was really easy for him to say this is a team deal. Some coaches say this is a team deal, but then tell everybody, 'I'm the head coach, and I can do whatever I want.'

"It's not just saying the words, it's about living the life and the actions you take. Players are smarter than they get credit for. You play the game with Coach Osborne and you get on the bus at 2 o'clock in the morning to go to the airport, and he's sitting there writing the game plan for next week. I mean, I don't even know if he sleeps. You always knew with him that he was putting in the time, too. It was pretty easy sacrificing for a team goal when you saw him doing it day in and day out."

Wiegert played for many coaches during his years of playing football, which included 12 years in the NFL. Osborne, above all others, had an incredible ability to connect with his players in a meaningful way. "He wasn't one of these guys who is so consumed with football all the time that he's not able to engage with the people around him. He was a very funny person; he had a dry sense of humor. He's the kind of guy who'll make fun of you in his office and 15 minutes later you catch the joke, and you realize he wasn't giving you a compliment, he was ripping on you," Wiegert says, laughing. It was this ability to connect that inspired Osborne's players to want to be at their best for him.

"The thing that still really sticks out about Coach Osborne even today is how he'll remember a guy who was a friend of mine that played when I did 20 years ago. He'll remember the guy's name. The guy was on the team for two years, but never played any downs, and he was on the freshman squad. But Coach Osborne will know everything about the guy. It's unbelievable. I'm not saying this to be arrogant, but my name is on the stadium because I won a major award, so it's pretty easy to remember me

(continued on next page)

as a player. The thing that impresses me is that the coach will remember guys that I played with, even though he hasn't seen them since we played. All of us felt that from him and still feel it to this day. It's easy to play hard for a man who does that."

In the end, Osborne doesn't measure his success as a coach by his career record of 255–49–3, 13 conference championships, and three national championships won in 1994, 1995, and 1997.

"Success always brings up a lot of different images," says Osborne, who celebrated his 75th birthday on February 23, 2012. "I think most people think of success in terms of how many games you won or how much money you made and those kinds of things. Certainly, I recognize that as a measure or standard, but I don't know that that's really how I ultimately would define success.

"I think John Wooden probably said it best, and I'm paraphrasing, when he said that success is doing the very best you can with what resources you've been given. Success really has to do with having a good work ethic, being of sound character, making sure that you try to be a person of your word, that if you say something you're going to do it. That you're trustworthy.

"And I think it's important to care about your employees, your players, the people that work under you, and try to make sure that they have the best possible outcomes, that you don't use them for your devices or purposes. Those would be some of the ways that I would define success. And that's what I tried to do during my coaching career, and even still today."

BRAD STEVENS: Focusing on the Journey

Brad Stevens was hired as the head basketball coach at Butler at age 30 in 2007, and since that time he's won more games his first three seasons than any coach in NCAA history. Through the 2010–11 season, Stevens sported a staggering overall win-loss record of 117–25 (82% winning percentage). Two of those losses came in consecutive NCAA national championship games, the journeys by which captured Butler legions of fans throughout the country. Now Stevens is one of the brightest stars in all of coaching.

While not surprised by his team's level of success, Stevens is confident that he would not have predicted it and remains humble in the face of it. "I don't think I could have dreamed it, because I still don't think I'm that good at it, but I just don't think you see yourself in that position and being able to coach guys at that level. The funny thing is, it is so much more normal once you get in the middle of it."

People want to know what is so special about Brad Stevens. How has he been able to do what he's done with the Butler basketball program?

For starters, he employs many of the coaching strategies outlined in previous chapters, as his players have attested. He is also well aware of his talents and spends time developing and utilizing his own unique set of strengths.

Stevens is a lifelong learner. When he reflects on his college basketball days as a reserve guard, he talks about the valuable lesson he learned when his playing time decreased as his college career progressed. Though challenged by the situation, he eventually made the choice to accept a different supporting role on his team. He is quick to point out that he is a better coach today thanks to this experience at DePauw University.

"[Playing less every season] was hard for me to handle during my junior year, and I didn't do a very good job handling it. That's when I coached a little youth team because I did an internship that summer, and I thought that gave me great perspective. In retrospect, I think I had a decision to make in my senior year. I had to decide if I was going to struggle with things I couldn't control or try to be as good a teammate as I could be. It wasn't easy, but it was something that I think was really beneficial down the line. I wouldn't

(continued on next page)

trade my college basketball experience for anything, because it made me a better coach."

In college, Stevens learned that the team has to supersede the individual. He applies this concept to himself as a coach as well, always giving credit elsewhere, and he expects this of every single one of his team members. He instills this lesson deeply into the hearts and minds of his Butler team. "I want to always bring credit to Butler and the game and this state. I told our guys this morning after a team workout, 'There are some expectations in this state, and they are: you play for the team, and you do so with a blue-collar attitude.' And I believe that. That's something our guys have done, and I think that's what made it intriguing to some people outside of the state of Indiana."

Growing up in Indiana, it may have been inevitable that Stevens would be a student of the game as a child. He spent a lot of time shooting around and playing with friends. Stevens's first legitimate classroom was the basketball goal he received.

"I vividly remember the day. It was my eighth birthday, and there was a basketball goal in my driveway. A lot of my better days during my childhood were not only about playing basketball but being a part of a team, whether it was little league baseball or basketball all the way through college. The other sports you play and the friendships you develop are important. That's all I did. Me and my buddy mowed some lawns, but we never mowed after noon. That's when we went and found an open court. We usually shot or played or created our own game."

Stevens is still a student of the game as an adult. In addition to being an avid reader, he learns as much as he can from other coaches in order to help his team members develop as people both on and off the court.

"Coaching is so hard. For seven years, I had gone back and forth, asking myself, is this what you want to do for the rest of your life? What you keep coming back to are the guys and how much fun it is to be around them and to be a part of higher education. Without question, if you can point to anything it would be the people I've been surrounded by. The first person I roomed with on the road and the first person I was assigned to do any administrative work for was Todd Lickliter [former Butler head coach who left to become head coach at Iowa; currently he's an assistant coach at Miami, Ohio]. Here I am, not only working for a good basketball mind, but more than that, a really good person who believed in empowering people and would only operate with integrity. There are no ifs, ands, or buts about it. He is one of the most honest and upright guys, and I hope that as more 22-year-olds get into this profession, they see this kind of person in the office instead of someone who'll steer them in the wrong direction."

When asked about the advice he doles out to other young men or women thinking of getting into coaching, he says he doesn't like to give that kind of advice, because each person has to make that decision for him, or herself. However, he still typically takes the time to share a little wisdom based on the lessons he's learned so far.

"You have to get in it for the right reasons. That's number one. You have to be a good mentor and value the relationships with your staff and your players. Whether you are the head coach or the assistant coach, value working together as a team. Number two, represent the school that you work for well. I think that's probably the way we define success here. People have really almost been taken aback and mad at me when I say that we don't have tangible goals of winning a championship, of going to a Final Four, or winning the National Championship. It's more about the process.

"One of the books that I've really paid attention to is *The Score Takes Care of Itself* by Bill Walsh [three-time Super Bowl–winning head coach of the San Francisco 49ers], which is an unbelievable book about focusing on the process. It also talks about the pitfalls of wanting more, and how hard it is when you get to a certain level to just want more and to always want to build, build, build, grow, grow, grow. It's human nature. It's the way things work. But my big deal is: focus on the journey, focus on the steps it takes to get there, and become the best that you can be."

Again, Stevens is a lifelong learner. Gleaning knowledge from coaches who have been successful is a key strategy for making the most of his learning strength. He takes time to study them and finds ways to allow their teachings to inform his coaching approach.

"I think the two coaches outside of the Butler family that I've tried to study the most or that I try to emulate are John Wooden and Tony Dungy. I do think I get a lot out of that cross-sport study. I believe football is an unbelievable sport to study because of what they have to do to manage the amount of staff and everything else. It makes basketball seem pretty simple."

Stevens is a self-professed "numbers guy." With an eye for details and

(continued on next page)

a mind for analyzing data, he realizes this is one of his strengths and has found a myriad of ways to use it to his advantage. From scouting opponents to making adjustments to his starting five, he relies on numbers to help his team put its best foot forward. Right out of college, his talent for analyzing numbers helped him land a plum job with Eli Lilly, a Fortune-500 pharmaceutical company. He continued to develop his skill as a lifelong learner at the company, picking up several transferrable skills that he now uses with his basketball program.

"I was 21 years old, right before my senior year in college. Eli Lilly offered me a job and I didn't say no. I accepted it and a lot of people I knew growing up had great careers at Lilly when it was thriving and the stock market was booming. They were living very comfortable lives and I liked that idea, but I wasn't ready for it at that age. I was in a unique position. Because of my internship, I was able to get the position, but I didn't work with a lot of people my age, so it's not like I came in with a large group fresh out of college. I worked with a lot of terrific people that I'm thankful for because they taught me how to be a professional in the corporate world. I think a lot of coaches don't get that experience.

"There were two main parts of my job: basically, 75 percent of it was coming up with how we were going to measure the performance of account executives with regard to their big sales, HMO, and things like that. I wasn't directly dealing with the sales people. I was doing metrics and incentives for those account executives. In the other part of my job, I was basically in charge of, or prepared and coordinated, large meetings. Those were the two things I did. That was a really interesting part of it, because team travel was easy after that. Except my budget was a little different."

Later, Stevens relied on numbers again to make an important career decision, calculating how long he could live off his savings account so he could leave Eli Lilly and take a volunteer coaching job at Butler. He was led by his heart but analyzed the numbers as insurance.

"I had worked camps since I was a freshman in college, so that's how I knew all the Butler guys. I had been there for 12 weeks over the course of four years, so I knew those guys before the summer I started at Lilly. I didn't start until August 2nd. I wanted golf money, so I just worked at the camp, and I ended up really liking it. A meeting with [former Butler and current Ohio State head coach] Thad Matta ended up being my big chance. First of all,

I'm spoiled. I was brought up in a house where we never struggled for food. We never struggled for lodging. My parents worked really hard. I was lucky because I wasn't as concerned about finances as I should have been. Because of that, I was able to save a lot of the money I had made at Lilly. I at least had a small savings account with money to lean on. I had a couple of buddies who let me move into a smaller room right down the road from Butler. I was paying about 300 bucks a month. I thought, I'm going to work camps in the summer and try to get a job waiting tables or whatever. I actually had a job lined up at Applebee's. I got fortunate, because I was hired as the director of basketball ops at Butler for about 30 grand less than I was making at Lilly, so it was great. I was the happiest guy in the world. It was enough to live on, and it wasn't enough to live on beyond frozen pizza and ramen noodles, but it was as much fun as I've had in this profession, that's for sure."

When it comes to his decisions, they are analyzed with numbers and made with the big picture in mind. That's another key strength that Stevens brings to the table as a man and a coach. He sees the big picture. That vision helped Stevens choose to attend DePauw University — he wanted to attend a school where he could be himself, a school that would prepare him for life.

"I didn't really have a lot of scholarship offers. I had one scholarship offer at the Division I level and maybe a couple at Division II. I don't remember, but I had some walk-on opportunities at some bigger schools. As I started to think about choosing a school, I felt the most important reasons should be: are you comfortable, and what's it going to do for you 40 years down the road? I think that gets lost in the shuffle. I've asked every recruit who's been in our office, 'What's most important to you?' and more often than not that's not the answer — but it probably should be. I think we all get swayed and we all get excited about the bright lights and the fancy stuff that everybody puts in their buildings and offices and the way they try to maximize their facilities, so they do capture your attention. But, golly, that's not a reason to go to school someplace. I think that's something I learned when I was choosing to go to DePauw. It turned out to be a good decision. Not every day was a great day, but I think that's another sign of a good decision — when you feel good about it on tough days and good days alike."

The big picture has also helped Stevens use his fear of failure as a driving force without letting it overtake him. Life is more than basketball. It's never as good as it seems, and it's never as bad as it seems. Being the person you want to be is what truly counts.

(continued on next page)

"What the fear of failure does for me is it puts me even more on alert to try to be better next time. I think that's what I'm trying to do. One of the things I've learned in coaching is that you really learn perspective. I handle losing a lot better now than when I was 20. I handle it way better than my five-year-old does, because I know all that goes into it. The other team is trying to beat you. Sometimes, you can do everything you want to do and it still doesn't go your way. That's why we all lose our hair.

"You do learn the important things. When people are offering their opinions on how you're doing your job, especially when things aren't going well, you realize how much you, your staff, and your players and you put into it, and that there are bigger things in life. Maybe that does help as you're going through all of it. I think that achieving all [that our team has] is nice, but it doesn't really define us. I think we go back to who we want to be on a daily basis. In James Allen's book *As a Man Thinketh*, he said, 'Men attract not that which they want, but that which they are.' You've got something, you've done it, but are you going to be it? You can talk about it. Are you going to do it again and again and again? That's something that we spend a lot of time talking about with our players.

"I think my fear of failure has gotten better over time. If you don't have perspective and you can't figure out the big picture in this business, then you're in trouble. I'm blessed to have people around me that keep me doing what I do in good and bad times. Without the right guys, without the right mindset, without the right approach, I don't think our team would have been able to turn it around last year, and they did.

"The losses, we'll get through those. It's one of those things where people of good character respond well to adversity. I think the hardest part is responding to success. I think it's hard to win. It's hard to be great. It's easy to rest on your laurels. It's easy to feel good about yourself. But as I've said, I've always been wired with a small fear of failure. When we finish the National Championship game, I'm thinking about how we're going to guard somebody in our league next year. That's just the way that some of us are wired, and that's the way I'm wired.

"It's the whole good-to-great concept and why some companies never truly become great. I read a book last summer, *How the Mighty Fall* by Jim Collins. It was really good because it says it's very easy to stick your chest out and talk about how good you are. The reason good-to-great doesn't happen very often is because human nature doesn't allow it. How can you combat that?

"Last year we went into the season saying, 'Your greatest opponent is human nature. Forget about everybody else.' That was something that was good in retrospect, but it did take us some time to understand what that meant, because it was hard being targeted. Next year [2011–12], we'll be targeted with no reason. Our freshmen didn't earn any of this. They think they're the beneficiary of it. Wait until they start playing other teams. We'll see.

"I love coaching. I love the challenges of it. I love the different unique challenges that come with it. I love the fact that next year we'll probably lose two more fringe-NBA players, and we'll see if we can win anyway. I love that. That's something that really drives me.

"I just like being around good people. I've always thought that. That's the thing about Butler. Just like our team and our staff are on one page, I really feel like our administration and leadership are on one page with us. We don't want to be a university and a basketball team. We want to be a university with a basketball team. I think we share very similar values, and we are on one track, going in one direction."

A thirst for learning. A calculating mind. The big-picture approach. These strengths rest on top of Stevens's consistent caring nature, direct communication, and demand that every team member puts the team first. Is it still a surprise that Butler's program has attained a high level of success? It shouldn't be.

Endnotes

p. 23

1. Jon Vaden, "Attaway Frosty," *2003 NCAA Division 3 Football Championship* magazine.

p. 37

2. Austin Murphy, "The Nicest Team in Football," *Sports Illustrated*, August 14, 2000.
3. Vaden, "Attaway Frosty."
4. Blaine Newnhan, "The Power of Positive Coaching – Happy Happy, Joy Joy, Hut Hut" *The Seattle Times,* November 20, 1994

p. 38

5. Vaden, "Attaway Frosty."

p. 39

6. Ibid.
7. Ibid.
8. Ibid.

p. 40

9. Fox Sports Net, *"The Slant"* video footage (2).
10. Vaden, "Attaway Frosty."

p. 68

1. Ivan Maisel, "Gould's Game," *Stanford Magazine*, www.stanfordalumni.org/news/magazine/1999/marapr/articles/tennis.html
2. Ibid.
3. Ibid.

p. 69

4. Bob Bryan interview, September 9, 2005, ASAP Sports, www.asapsports.com/show_interview.php?id=3847
5. Greg Garber, "Jailed Tanner's losses: Game, set, match . . . family," ESPN.com, sports.espn.go.com/sports/tennis/news/story?id=2491460
6. Ivan Maisel, "Gould's Game."

p. 70

7. Eric Konigsberg, "Unseparated Since Birth," *New York Times,* August 24, 2009, www.nytimes.com/2009/08/30/magazine/30brothers-t.html

p. 83

1. John McEnroe with James Kaplan, *You Cannot Be Serious* (New York: Putnam, 2003) p. 78.

p. 107

1. en.wikipedia.org/wiki/Paul_Goldstein_(tennis)
2. Ivan Maisel, "Gould's Game."
3. Casey Angle, "The Last Dynasty: A Look Back at Stanford's Perfect '98 Season," October 9, 2008, www.itatennis.com/Page1761.aspx
4. Ibid.

p. 124

5. Jon Vaden, "Attaway Frosty," *2003 NCAA Division 3 Football Championship* magazine.
6. Doug Drowley, "Pulling Together," *The News Tribune* (Tacoma, WA).
7. Vaden, "Attaway Frosty."
8. Drowley, "Pulling Together."

p. 125

9. Ibid.

p. 126

10. Ibid.
11. Blaine Newnhan, "The Power of Positive Coaching – Happy Happy, Joy Joy, Hut Hut," *The Seattle Times.*

p. 127

12. Vaden, "Attaway Frosty."

p. 152

1. S.L. Price, "Anson Dorrance," *Sports Illustrated,* December 7, 1998.
2. Anson Dorrance and Gloria Averbuch, *The Vision of a Champion* (Huron River Press, Ann Arbor, MI, 2005), in www.championshipcoachesnetwork.com/public/400.cfm
3. S.L. Price, "Anson Dorrance."
4. Tim Crothers, *The Man Watching* (New York: St. Martin's, 2010), p. 96.
5. Dorrance and Averbuch, *The Vision of a Champion,* www.championshipcoachesnetwork.com/public/400.cfm
6. Graham Hays, "Numbers tell only half the story of UNC soccer coach's legacy,"ESPN.com, sports.espn.go.com/ncaa/columns/story?columnist=hays_graham&id=2924051

p. 158

7. www.dangable.com/bio/
8. YouTube "Dan Gable Part 6 - Coach Gable," http://www.youtube.com/watch?v=zBryGcA9JNw
9. Ibid.
10. Ibid.
11. Ibid.